The
Spiritual
Girl's
Guide to Dating

YOUR ENLIGHTENED PATH
TO LOVE, SEX,
& SOUL MATES

Amy Leigh Mercree
CONSCIOUS DATING COACH

Aadamsmedia
AVON, MASSACHUSETTS

Published by
Adams Media, a division of F+W Media, Inc.
57 Littlefield Street, Avon, MA 02322. U.S.A.
www.adamsmedia.com

ISBN 10: 1-4405-2980-9
ISBN 13: 978-1-4405-2980-1
eISBN 10: 1-4405-3029-7
eISBN 13: 978-1-4405-3029-6

Printed in the United States of America.

10   9   8   7   6   5   4   3   2   1

Library of Congress Cataloging-in-Publication Data
is available from the publisher.

This book is available at quantity discounts for bulk purchases.
For information, please call 1-800-289-0963.

Dedication

For my amazing husband, who makes every day even
more magical. I love you.

Acknowledgments

So much love and teamwork goes into turning a seed of an idea into a beautiful book. Thanks go to Dr. Laurie Nadel, who followed her intuition and helped a sister out. To my lovely, kind agent, Lisa Hagan, thank you for believing in this book.

Major gratitude to the crew at Adams Media, who midwifed this book into being: Paula Munier, you said yes and answered my many questions with a spirit of fun imbued with the joy of books. Katie Corcoran Lytle, Meredith O'Hayre, Mathew Glazer, Chris Duffy, Suzanne Goraj, and Jane Hauptman, thank you for all of your help. Through her coaching and literary finesse, a readable and organized book was born thanks to editor extraordinaire Jennifer Lawler.

Clients, friends, and spiritual women everywhere: Thank you for your stories. You inspire me to write. I honor each and every one of you and your personal journeys of evolution.

Lastly, my wonderful family and friends—thank you all so much for your steadfast support, especially my parents, husband, and brother.

Contents

Introduction

Getting Started with Spiritual Dating

True or false:

1. You're not trying to "get a man." You're trying to find a potential life partner to connect with, someone who is as mindful and open as you are.
2. You're not interested in playing games with the men you meet, pretending to like things you don't, or toning down your personality so that you don't scare a guy off.
3. Whether you choose to wear nail polish, lipstick, and/or painful shoes has nothing to do with whether you're going on a date.

Did you pick "true" for each answer? Then you've come to the right place. If you're tired of dating by the rules, *The Spiritual Girl's Guide to Dating* is for you!

Spiritual dating is your ticket to a happy, fulfilling love life. It honors you and respects you as a human being and as a spiritual being. Spiritual dating is the emotionally healthy way of dating as a conscious, empowered woman. It is a dating philosophy that this book teaches you how to put into action in your life.

WHAT YOU'LL LEARN

By reading this book and becoming a spiritual dater, you can expect to embark on a journey of self-awareness to heal past hurts and to open your heart in a safe and manageable way. Then, you'll learn how to set the intention to attract your soul mate, or whomever you would like to date. You will strengthen yourself in the process and become the magnetic catch you are meant to be.

Next, you will understand the process of manifesting your ideal dates, all the while learning to keep your third eye (intuition) wide open. Savvy and sexy, you will become prepared with the knowledge you need to flourish in the dating world.

Then, you'll explore intimacy and sacred sexuality. You will learn of a new sexual paradigm that values your beautiful, sacred soul. Ultimately, you'll arrive at the destination of lovingkindness toward yourself and your dates. You'll experience an emotionally healthy dating life that is fulfilling and fun.

NOT JUST FOR GIRLS!

Men can benefit from reading *The Spiritual Girl's Guide to Dating*, too. They can read it with a mind to finding their spiritual partner. They need to get emotionally mature and ready to meet their soul mate. Some of the self-awareness exercises in the book can help them achieve that.

Men who love spiritual women can read this book and understand spiritual dating to help their best friends, nieces, sisters. And they just might learn something amazing for themselves along the way.

A LOVE NOTE TO OUR GAY, LESBIAN, AND BISEXUAL READERS

We love you! This book is for you. Almost all the information in here applies to same-gender relationships, dating, and sex. When we talk about sex and intercourse specifically, for our gay and bisexual readers, it can also be any equivalent act.

Most of the relationship information in the book pertains to gay as well as heterosexual relationships. Some gender characteristics may be a bit different, but the rest is the same.

I endorse and support all kinds of love among all people. Love and passion are beautiful in all of their harmonious forms.

ABOUT THE STORIES

Throughout the book, you'll find stories of people pursuing spiritual dating to help show what the practices look like in action. Many of them are anecdotes from clients and friends over the years. Sometimes I have combined multiple clients' stories into one or emphasized one part of the story to illustrate the story's lesson. All names and identifying details have been changed to protect everyone's privacy. The stories about me are, of course, mostly straightforward accounts of my experiences.

HOW THE BOOK CAME INTO BEING

As a medical intuitive and conscious dating coach for more than ten years, I have seen many women and men struggle with dating in alignment with their hearts. I have witnessed the emotional and physical ailments associated with not honoring ourselves in our dating lives. It became clear to me over the years that a new paradigm in dating was needed. I call it spiritual dating; sometimes, I also call it sacred dating.

I watched my clients' lives get better when they chose spiritual dating. At the same time, I decided to live it and immerse myself in what it looked and felt like. I made plenty of missteps along the way. Some of the principles of spiritual dating were harder than others for me to put into practice. It might be the same for you, too. Ultimately, I got it right. I learned to value myself, nurture my authenticity, open my heart, and have fun doing it. Then, at thirty-two, I met my wonderful, amazing, magical husband. And the rest is the usual happy ending with an extra special spiritual twist.

I know this system works. That's why I feel confident in inviting you to get ready to become a spiritual dater!

Part One

Open Your Heart

In this part, you'll learn why opening your heart is a necessary step in spiritual dating. When you open your heart, you feel more love and experience life more fully. You live your authentic truth.

In the following chapters, you'll learn to build and enhance your self-concept as a step toward making spiritual dating work for you. You'll learn to make choices about what is best for you.

And you'll learn that any impediment to an open heart can be dissolved with love. You'll find out how to clear away the old painful patterns, past hurts, and limited beliefs to open yourself to a gorgeous future of happiness and pleasure.

Sound good? Then let's get started!

Chapter One
Spiritual Dating

If you're like most women, you would love to have a happy romantic life, but you've found that dating is a hard way to get there. While dating can be fun, it can also be tiresome and saddening, especially if you've been burned by someone you've dated. You have probably felt that there must be a better way. There is! Spiritual dating is a way to date and enjoy yourself that is emotionally safer, gentler, and infinitely more pleasurable than regular dating.

Spiritual dating allows you to find the soul mate the universe wants you to find and to create a loving, stable relationship that will support and nourish you. Spiritual dating is about attracting others through the fullest expression of your inner self, not through superficial appearances. It gives you a strong foundation of self-love and self-respect from which to create your ideal dating life. It helps you attract loving perfection into your life.

What Is Loving Perfection?

Loving perfection isn't perfect! Perfection, in this case, doesn't imply a partner or a relationship that is perfect with no flaws. It means your version of what will be just right and best for you personally. It is going to be different for each person.

Figuring out what is ideal for you in your dating life will make it much easier to set your sights on what you want—and to get it. Here is an example: Allison dated a string of men she thought were right for her. Each had the high-end clothes, the high-powered job, the handsome appearance. When she sat down to figure out what her heart actually wanted, she realized her ideal was already in her life—her good friend Jack, a veterinarian who also managed an animal shelter. He was cute and real. He listened and was always there for her. Was he glamorous? No way. But his kindness and caring were just what Allison was looking for. Luckily, he was single and harboring a secret crush on her. And so Allison and Jack lived loving perfection together!

SPIRITUAL DATING

Spiritual Dating has six essential components:

- Deep respect for yourself and others
- Authentic behavior
- Desire to grow
- Empowered sense of self-love
- Commitment to your own enjoyment and pleasure
- Dancing, playing, expansive fun

Let's look at each of these important components.

DEEP RESPECT FOR YOURSELF AND OTHERS

Deeply respecting yourself is the first step toward having a deep respect for others. If you can love yourself and forgive your failings, then you can do the same for others as well. Feel that respect for all life by reminding yourself that you are perfect just as you are.

Expand that respect to the world around you: Notice and respect the beautiful flower, the bee that is pollinating it, the flawed radiance of a family member. Each moment, each person, is sacred and worthy of respect—especially you.

Start with yourself and respecting the sacredness of others will follow. When dating, remember to be aligned with this idea of deeply respecting yourself and your dates, simply because they exist. Respect is the essential ingredient that takes dating from "normal" to spiritual. Respecting yourself means listening to your heart, body, mind, and spirit, and honoring them all. Flaws and strengths, they are all uniquely you and worthy of true respect.

Someone who doesn't respect herself demeans herself by saying things like "I'm so chubby and unattractive, no wonder I can't get a date." She may date a guy who doesn't treat her kindly and with the respect she deserves because she doesn't respect herself. She may sleep with the self-proclaimed players who are not interested in monogamy, thinking that is the best she can get even though she craves a loving heart connection and a true relationship.

Someone who doesn't respect herself will have difficulty respecting others. She may lie about her actions or whereabouts. She may cheat either literally or emotionally while in a relationship. She may set a date and not show up at all or even call. She may talk cruelly about someone behind his back while pretending to be a friend to his face. It is crucial to respect ourselves and others so we can move into the realm of spiritual dating and feel an integrity within ourselves.

AUTHENTIC BEHAVIOR

Authentic behavior grows from respecting yourself. It means acting in accordance with your beliefs and values, even when others disagree. Sometimes we have a hard time doing this. Have you ever kept your real feelings to yourself because you felt it was what you were "supposed" to do or because you felt you would be liked better?

For example, you meet your new guy's family and they all love bluegrass music. You hate it and think it sounds twangy and annoying. But you act as if you like it too because it's such a family bond and you want them to like you. For the next ten years, you get bluegrass CDs for your birthday and books about bluegrass for Christmas.

Or you are on a date with a guy who is very nice but you know this man is not your soul mate. You can feel it and your intuition is clear about it. He is talking of the future and seems to have really fallen for you. Is it kinder to be authentic and tell him how you are really feeling or to just dodge his calls till he gets the message? Obviously, to tell him kindly and directly. Strive for authenticity on your dates. It will make the interaction that much more honest and real—cornerstones of good friendships and relationships.

Being open to new experiences is great, but keep it real. Choose authenticity. Speak your mind. Express how you are really feeling—simply choose kindness as well and you will go far with your authentic life.

DESIRE TO GROW

The third component of spiritual dating is a desire to grow. This exists inside us all. In some, it is buried more deeply. In others, it blazes on the surface. In most of us, it is somewhere in between. Your desire to grow makes you intriguing and attractive. Your dates probably won't be able to put their finger on it, but it will fascinate them, nonetheless. A desire to grow consists of curiosity about the world, a drive to learn and become more self-aware. It is about striving to better your life and polish your being, from the surface to the depths, to a shining gleam. When you desire to grow as a person, you put effort into becoming your very best self. This is good for you! You are happier, more engaged, more interesting. You feel better and are more emotionally healthy and your heart is more open.

Stoke that fire of evolution. How can you foster it? You can look at what life brings up for you, the pain-in-the-ass coworker or the deeply affecting family situation, and work through it. Learn about yourself through it. With the pain-in-the-ass coworker, you can view the situation as an opportunity to grow. You might ask yourself:

- "How can I respect this person?"
- "How can I authentically express my feelings to the coworker and set appropriate boundaries in terms of being with this person?"
- "What are the gifts in this situation?"
- "What is it showing me about myself?"

In dating, you can grow through each dating experience. Instead of thinking "Well, that was a disaster," you can look at what happened and learn from it. Let's say you went on a first date with a guy you met on an online dating site. As the date progressed he revealed that he was recently unemployed. You'd never really asked him about his job. On his profile you liked how he looked and the fact that he was a fan of the band The Cure like you are. As the check arrived, he tried to convince you to "dine and dash." You were so offended! You paid and obviously didn't see him again. Instead of being negative about it and thinking, "What a jerk! I will never date an unemployed guy again!" you could look at ways to grow and learn from this experience. An obvious one would be asking more questions of potential online dates. What do they do for work? What are their values? You could notice that online dating is a great platform to get lots of info on a guy before even meeting him. Next time, you could use it to its fullest!

You can also spend time thinking about why you're attracted to certain kinds of men and why they are attracted to you. Are they your ideal? Or are you not attracting your ideal? More on this later, but for now, consider what isn't working in your dating relationships so that you can focus on what is.

You can especially keep your eyes open for the dates who also desire to grow; they might be keepers. Someone who desires to grow is curious, interested in learning new things and having new experiences. A guy who likes to grow will try new things such as going roller skating for the first time with you on a date. He might talk about cool news articles and admire people who are out-of-the-box thinkers.

EMPOWERED SENSE OF SELF-LOVE

An empowered sense of self-love means you truly love and accept yourself as you would a treasured lover or a sweet, wonderful child, and that you do this from a place of strength of character and belief in yourself. You can feel powerful in this love for yourself. You bring this with you everywhere you roam, and it is tantalizing to potential dates.

To foster this, affirm, "I am powerful in my love for myself. The truth of my being is I love myself exactly as I am. I honor my empowered heart."

COMMITMENT TO YOUR OWN ENJOYMENT AND PLEASURE

A commitment to your enjoyment and pleasure is exemplified by choosing activities and relationships that make you feel good. If they don't—at least most of the time—why are you there? You're not doing anyone any favors.

Likewise, dating should make you feel good. It should start out easily and enjoyably and build to the level of intensity you are most comfortable with. An eye to this truth from the beginning can inform you early about compatibility between you and a potential partner. When you are committed to your enjoyment and pleasure, you naturally let go of people and situations that consistently interfere with that. Because they don't bring you happiness and joy, you gently release them in the perfect way.

An example is dating someone who manipulates you into feeling low or depressed. He wants to drag you down to his level of happiness or lack thereof. When you commit to spiritual dating and your enjoyment and pleasure, you will be able to let that person go. You will have the courage to choose your happiness and feel worthy that it is important. You can set some guidelines for yourself around this topic, such as: "If a date is morose or a downer I will move on; if a date is crude or makes offensive jokes at my expense I will not see him again; if a date crosses my boundaries too soon or I feel uncomfortable I will refrain from dating him more."

On the other hand you can also commit to the following: "If a date and I have major fun and he is kind I will consider dating him again; if a date introduces me to a new activity that I really enjoy (like surfing) I will be grateful and consider it a plus for further dating; if a date is generally fun and prizes enjoyment and pleasure and is also kind and caring I will honor that in him and enjoy our time together."

A commitment to your enjoyment and pleasure puts you in the place of joy. Dating should feel that good. If it doesn't feel good, enjoyable, pleasurable, then you know you need to do something differently. Spiritual daters are looking to feel good in their bodies, spirits, hearts, and minds. They want the whole package and they don't settle for anything less.

DANCING, PLAYING, EXPANSIVE FUN

Dancing, playing, expansive fun just sounds good, doesn't it? Can you have it? Are you open to it? Start solo by going for a fun beach walk and run and play on the edge of the water between land and sea. Play at-home karaoke and sing along with your favorite songs in the mirror in the most wacky costume you can create from your closet in three minutes or less and rock out. Make a collage of the funniest images and words you can find in magazines and newspapers and theme it something like "pratfalls" or "girls on the brink of hysterical laughter."

Then try it with friends. Go on a timed five-minute shopping spree race at the thrift store for the most outrageous and crazy-looking costumes, put them on and then all go out for drinks at the town's stuffiest wine bar. Take a group hike and then a swim in a chilly mountain pool at the end. Have a goddesses dance party and invite all your girls (and their girls) to dance in your living room, give each other pedis, and then have ice cream sundaes.

Then try it on a date. If that date can hang with your fun self, he might be worth seeing again. The spirit of fun keeps your dating life interesting and not boring. Spiritual folks want to feel challenged and enjoy life. Spirituality is not serious! It is about being present, in the moment. And in this case, enjoying the moment. Spiritual dating requires you both to have the ability to stay present in the moment and expand together. Dancing, playing, and having fun can foster this in you both.

You can spiritually date today and you don't even need a date to do it! It is more about your attitude and your desire for more—more love, more fun, more pleasure, more enjoyment, more peak experiences, more vulnerability, more strength, more self-actualization. Live it now, date or not!

CREATE A JOYFUL YOU

If you take away nothing else from reading this guide, please take away the knowledge that *you* are the key. You are the magic code that unlocks your happiness. As architect of your reality, you are empowered to create it as you choose. You set the course of your existence—including your dating life. When you incorporate the six components of spiritual dating into your life, you can set your dating course toward joyful, spiritual, open hearted men.

If you are looking for happiness, as most of us are, then you need to set a strong course. Your compass must point toward joy. Imagine this compass made of energy. It exists in your heart, the center of your chest. Set your heart compass to joy by saying aloud, "I now set my heart compass firmly pointing me toward joy, forevermore. It is done."

With your course set, you have the beautiful opportunity to make conscious joyful choices. Life is going to provide you with wonderful choice points; the more you choose joy, the more joy will effortlessly come to you.

CHOOSE OPENNESS

One of the essences of human existence is choice. It is a vehicle for our growth and expansion. Celebrate it. Revel in your breadth of choices. They are fabulous and so are you, you joyful creature.

Opening your heart is your next step in spiritual dating. Opening your heart means valuing yourself, forgiving yourself, and letting life's lessons in. Learning is natural to human existence. Making mistakes is expected. Let yourself off the hook. Forgive when you have harmed yourself or another and move forward having learned from those experiences. Part of valuing yourself is recognizing your mistakes and accepting yourself because of, or in spite of, them.

To truly value yourself sometimes takes practice. You may have to engage in some loving self-talk. Here are a few exercises to get you started.

Wonderful You

What is something wonderful about you?

Anything at all?

Create a sentence that positively affirms that wonderful thing. For example, "I am great at making collages."

What is another wonderfulness about you? List at least four more. Write those wonderfulnesses on a small piece of paper and post it on your bathroom mirror. Once a week or more, create a new positive sentence and post it around the house: in the closet, on the refrigerator, wherever you feel compelled.

VALIDATE YOURSELF

You have the power to validate yourself. Often, we seek outside of ourselves for the world to give us the message that we are okay, that we are worth loving. Screw that! Claim your lovability and own it! You aren't perfect? So what! Neither is anyone else—newsflash!

1. State it aloud now: "I am lovable. I love myself. I validate myself. I trust myself. I live love." That is the most important step on your path to living loving perfection and opening your heart.

2. How do you live this truth: "I value myself"? *Act* like you value yourself. Choose actions and make decisions that demonstrate your value. Value your time and how you spend it. Be conscious about your actions and decisions. If you are faced with lots of friends and family wanting your time spent with them, instead of agreeing to a seemingly

endless string of social and familial obligations, choose the ones that matter most to you.

3. Your time and energy are important! Rather than washing cars at your neighborhood's car wash fundraiser for the local fire department, simply donate a bit of money with a heartfelt card of gratitude to the firefighters. Value your energy and how you use it.

4. Often, we need more time to recharge our batteries than we get. Valuing yourself means taking time to rejuvenate your body and spirit. Do you need more recharge time? How can you carve it out for yourself? Set boundaries. Take some time to list what is important to you. How do you want to spend your time? What are the top five ways you want to spend your time? Say no when something feels obligatory and you don't feel like doing it. Listen to your intuition. What feels right in these situations?

5. Men respond to how you value yourself. Many will act accordingly, showering you with affection and dates that are designed to be enjoyable to a hot ticket like yourself. Expect this! Settle for nothing less.

6. Look for honest, kind men who excite you with their passion. Go forth with a mind to valuing yourself and watch the results in your dating life.

OPEN YOUR HEART BY FOLLOWING NATURAL LAW

Spiritual dating functions best when done according to Natural Law. What is Natural Law? It simply means helping all and harming none. Each moment is an opportunity to choose love, to open your heart, and to learn to date spiritually.

By living Natural Law and choosing love in each moment, you line yourself up to attract and experience the same love and caring in return. Think how that can transform your dating life! No more sleazy guys disguised as potential dates. No more men seeking the next conquest without regard for you and who you are. Instead, the energy of helping all and harming none can pervade your life. You can easily avoid those duds and move into the clear, spiritual realm of conscious, evolved dating. If you want to date consciously, then live life helping all and never harming yourself or others. When you date according to Natural Law, something amazing happens; it is grace. You can relax into however your dates unfold, trusting yourself to know just what to do and what is right for you.

The other part of Natural Law is this: Whatever you put out, you receive back threefold. It is the Law of Three. So, in choosing loving-kindness, you set yourself up to receive it. It is an endless circle of win/win energy and you can step into it. Reap the dates and benefits of your good deeds sown.

Saying the phrase "I live love" to yourself is one way that you can steep yourself in the energy of Natural Law and thereby experience more of it. Go for it!

INVOKE NATURAL LAW

To enact Natural Law in your life, you must commit to it as best as you can. Then you must invoke it. To invoke Natural Law as a powerful force in your life, decree aloud, "I now choose to live Natural Law, for my highest good. I allow myself and life to transform and raise in vibration exponentially. I choose love in each moment. It is done."

It is done! So simple, isn't it? When we speak aloud, our bodies hear it and respond. Your body is designed to live Natural Law. It is perfectly calibrated for this. All you had to do was activate it. You can periodically restate the activation throughout your life to further strengthen your commitment to Natural Law.

MAKE RESPONSIBLE CHOICES

The intention to live Natural Law does not exempt you from making responsible choices. You are still in control of your existence. Natural Law–aligned choices will simply be highlighted for you. You must be conscious. You are the decider! You make the choice to live Natural Law in each moment.

PROPER UNIVERSAL ALIGNMENT

To further attune yourself toward self-love and valuing yourself as you are, you can use a technique that brings you into proper universal alignment with all existence. This includes your body, heart, mind, spirit. Try it. It is simple.

Out loud, say three times: "Proper universal alignment. Proper universal alignment. Proper universal alignment." Feel your spine align as you say this and notice any bodily feelings or sensations. Say it as frequently as you feel inspired. It only helps and never harms; Natural Law is built into it.

When we heal and align our beings, we feel safer and healthier, which allows us to become spiritual daters. Our bodies feel better, we feel happier, and we are more attractive to potential dates. Proper universal alignment feels good. It inspires our growth and safety. It fosters our spirit of well-being. More total alignment with self and life translates into deeper connection with the sacred, the divine. Connection with sacredness in ourselves and our universe inspires feelings of well-being, of belonging, of purpose, of happiness. We then feel safer to open our hearts!

With dating, if you are existing in proper universal alignment, then you are far ahead of the game. You will attract better quality dates. You will also be empowered to make choices that affirm your life.

Have faith in yourself and your ability to make conscious, healthy decisions for yourself. I have that faith in you, because you are here to grow, reading this book and choosing to better yourself. That is why I know you will not only be okay, you will flourish. It is done!

URSULA'S VALUE

Ursula's life had become a series of obligations. Family demands, social demands, work demands, Ursula was exhausted by it all. She needed to prioritize her life. She needed to value herself above others. To do that, she had to decide what was important to her. She hadn't asked herself that in a long time.

MAKING COMMITMENTS

She took a whole weekend for herself—unheard-of for her in the past. She turned off her cell phone, didn't check her e-mail, and stopped answering her door. She thought back to before she took her stable job in finance. In college, she was a good painter and an even better sculptor. That felt important, so she decided to make a commitment to herself: Do art at least once per week.

Commitment one. Check.

Next, she looked at how she spent her time. She was blessed with a large extended family who all lived in neighboring towns but she needed time to relax and—novel idea—date on her weekends off. She decided she would go to two family events per month. She could decide which ones at the beginning of each month and if impromptu ones arose, she would be unavailable except under extenuating circumstances or if she really wanted to go because it would be fun.

Commitment two. Check.

Next, her friends. She loved them. She wanted to see them in doses that worked for her. She decided she wouldn't simply agree with all social plans. She would value her time for creativity and recharging. About once a week she would see her friends. She'd be flexible but keep in mind her priorities of creativity and recharging. This felt good to her. So much less pressure!

Commitment three. Check.

Now, what to do with the free time? Ursula sank deeply into herself and asked, "How do I want to spend my time?" She answered, "Doing art, learning guitar, meeting kind guys, socializing for fun not obligation, being quiet." Ursula happily wrote up her notes to refer to later.

SPIRITUAL DATING

Ursula hadn't started this process specifically to improve her love life, but by paying attention to the six components that create a happy, spiritual life, she found herself spiritually dating! Remember, the six components that create a happy, spiritual life are the same ones that create spiritual dating.

As Ursula became more proficient about valuing herself, she signed up for the guitar lessons she had been wanting to take for years. She loved it. After she'd been taking lessons for a while, the guitar instructor said to her, "You are really talented for someone who has only been seriously playing for five months." Something in the way they looked at each other made her think he was attracted to her—as she was to him. She wondered if it would be okay to flirt with him. Before she said anything, he suggested that she move to another class with a different instructor.

"You can get more fundamental knowledge suited to your talent that way. And then, I wouldn't be your teacher."

"Oh," she said a bit shyly and slightly stunned. "Is there a reason you don't want to be my teacher, Carl?" she hinted with a smile.

"Yes. But I can't ask you till you aren't my student."

"Okay, I am officially no longer your student," Ursula decided with surety.

Carl's breath rushed out in relief, "Whew, that was nerve-racking. Would you like to go out Friday night?"

"Yes, I would."

Ursula smiled as she thought back to that pivotal night when she decided to value herself. It was a good decision.

HEART EXPANSION

Imagine your heart, your emotional center, forever expanding. It transcends you. It is eternal. Infinite. Even divine in nature. What do you imagine might inspire you to open up your heart this way? How could you let greater levels of heart expansion happen for you? Think back to times when you have felt your heart swell with love. Those moments expand your emotional capacity. Experiences move us. People and their caring and actions affect us. Sometimes it happens because we intend it to. Sometimes it is a surprise, a gift to light our way.

Be open to these experiences. Start with the nonromantic ones if you are skittish from being hurt too many times. Life provides chances to open your heart all the time. Pay attention to them and take advantage of their beauty. Your life will be enhanced overall and your love life will morph into the blooming, radiant string of experiences it is meant to be.

Chapter Two
Processing the Past to Create a Radiant Present

Sometimes after years of ups and downs, relationships, marriages, lonely times and joyful times, we are overwhelmed with emotional baggage—good and bad. Baggage is not innately negative; it's just a product of our experiences. It's when the baggage gets in the way of our happiness and living our lives to the fullest that we have to handle it. We have to put it down.

Opening your heart and improving your dating life requires you to take steps to work through your personal baggage. Without undergoing this process, you create more of the same dating situations that created some of the baggage in the first place. Processing your life, from childhood to now, takes attention and intention. You have to want to grow and expand through your heart and your psyche. You have to want more for yourself—more love, more heart, more truth, more authenticity, and more self-awareness. *Lots* more self-awareness.

CREATE SELF-AWARENESS

Knowing what motivates your behavior in matters of the heart is one of the most important steps you can take toward spiritual dating. This chapter is going to help you mine that knowledge.

To get started, you need the willingness to:

- Go deep. Really open yourself to seeing your patterns, delusions, and what you want to make better.
- Apply yourself to this level of self-awareness knowing that it will enhance your quality of life forevermore. In other words, make a commitment.
- Choose courage as you face your past. Own it. It made you who you are.
- Reap all of your past's gifts. All the hurt, the fun, the anger, the joy, the sadness, the love, the betrayal, the honoring—receive every last gift from it all.

HOW PROCESSING WORKS

Processing means analyzing your experiences to determine why you made the choices you did. In some ways, our bodies, minds, and hearts are like sophisticated, organic computers with all kinds of internal processors. Some parts of the machine take years to do their jobs, some take seconds. To some degree, processing our thoughts and emotions happens unconsciously all the time.

When we apply our conscious focus to this process, we accelerate the speed at which we can move forward emotionally and cognitively. All this takes is the intention to be self-aware and keep growing. You can set the intention now to learn from your past and move forward in strength and open-hearted beauty. Some intentions you could set are: "I choose to consciously learn from my experiences to move forward, making choices that are increasingly more positive and pleasurable for me. I am a fast and thorough learner and grower; my life keeps getting better and better because of it!"

LEARN FROM YOUR DATING PAST

Looking at your past experiences and choices can help you define what you do and do not want to choose in your life. Your past can teach you what works for you (and what does not) and can help you make conscious choices.

By taking time after the fact to process what has happened, you can paint a picture of how your emotions and choices have defined you in the past and thereby consciously create the future you choose. Throughout the book, we will discuss topics such as how who you have slept with might be affecting your pocketbook and constructive ways to identify the warning signs of your negative relationship patterns. One of the first steps in this process of making over your dating life is becoming more self-aware. There is no judgment here. You made choices that shaped you and you might choose to make different ones in the future. We are just exploring options and noticing for now.

Dating patterns emerge quickly for some of us. The classic "she likes bad boys" observation exemplifies a simple and easy-to-see pattern. For some of us, it is just that simple: We realize we are not happy with bad boys and set the intention of seeking out relationships with men who are solid, authentic, and reliable. But for most of us, our negative patterns are more subtle. Looking closely at our choices can help suss out these tendencies.

EXAMINE YOUR PAST RELATIONSHIPS

To begin, take a few minutes and reflect on your long-term relationships and dating history. Breathe deeply and feel yourself relax with each breath in and out. Let go of your worries and inhibitions and just allow yourself to be present in the moment. See a visual image in your mind of yourself smiling and happy.

What does that look like? Feel it in your heart. Make a commitment to yourself that you will analyze your life and relationships to get you there!

1. List your long-term dating and married relationships in order on a sheet of paper. Leave some space in between each one for notes. If you're so inclined, you can make a chart.

   - Now, starting from your earliest relationship, go down the list and write three keywords that would best describe what attracted you to that person.
   - Next, go down the list again and write a few keywords about why you think the relationship didn't work out.
   - Start at the top again and list what parts of the relationship not working out you feel were the other person's fault.
   - Next, list how you contributed to that relationship's downfall.
   - Now, take a few minutes to reflect on your close parental or caretaker relationships from childhood. Start a parental relationships list on the same paper. Did you have a positive relationship with your parents? Were your emotional (and other) needs met in these relationships?
   - How do your parental relationships shape your current romantic relationships? For example, if your father was not around much or withheld validation, do you notice that you are choosing partners who do the same?
   - Next, look at each romantic relationship on your list and ask if it has an echo of one of your parental or close adult relationships. Some examples might be: emotional unavailability, lack of affection, explosive angry outbursts, a happy loving partnership, a caring connection, feeling stifled or overly needed.

- Now, reread all of your notes and consider what your past partners have in common. Write about that. Are you surprised by the results? Were you expecting them? Is a pattern emerging? You may notice that all of your partners showed a strong dominant side to their personalities. If so, look at your parental relationships. Another example is ending up with guys who need your help. Look at why that shows up in your life. Can you trace the reason for that? Do one or both of your parents tend to favor the underdog, even to their detriment?

- In light of your answer to the previous question, what needs within you were you trying to fill by choosing the partners you did? If, for example, you are a woman who chose a dominant partner, did you have a belief on some level that if your parent loves you they will be dominant and controlling and so you sought out those types of boyfriends? You were trying to fill a need to feel loved but it never really satiated your hunger for love because it was a false sense of love, not the real thing. If your past shows you are the underdog-helper, did you internalize that you are only a good person if you help others? Were you trying to fill a need to feel worthy, but because it never came from within (instead it came from external actions), you never felt that you were good enough?

  You can recognize your patterns by looking at the subtle details that were off somehow, especially the overarching emotional themes in your relationships. Pay special attention to the problems and points of contention. What did not work? How did things not feel right with each partner? What were the most common feelings: shame, doubt, anger, sadness, depression, disappointment?

- Next, look at your parents' or adult role models' romantic relationships. What are they like and what were they like during your formative child and teen years? Were your parents affectionate toward each other? Were they connected and close? Angry or hostile? Was one waiting by the phone for the other? Was one submissive and one controlling? Or did they battle for control in a passionate battle of wills? Do the romantic relationships of your role models have anything in common with yours?

- Look at your choices with a mind to understanding why you made them. Choose to be even more aware of future choices. List the patterns you have enacted in your relationships and where they may have come from. Ask yourself what conscious and unconscious places they came from. Write any thoughts about that. Ultimately, what do you want to let go of to make room for newer, healthier patterns?

In the act of examining your past, you can begin to bring to light things that you are ready to release from your way of being. You may not always be clear on your patterns; sometimes they take time to work out. Ultimately, if your intention is to release what no longer serves you to make room for greater levels of love and joy in your life, that is what will happen.

LETTING GO

Letting go is the act of allowing what no longer serves you to dissolve or wash away. It is *allowing;* there is little effort beyond your intention in the actual letting go. You are ready to let go of unhealthy patterns and so you will. It is easy, if you let it be.

Relax into the idea that letting go is really a loosening of these old patterns. They unwind as you look at them and feel any related feelings. They simply fall away as you let them.

Give yourself permission to embark on this journey of letting go. Know that it may take minutes or years but trust that it will be just right. Love yourself for making this choice. Many people choose stagnation. You are courageous! Pat yourself on the back and give yourself a hug! You are doing a great job of growing and expanding.

LETTING-GO EXERCISE

To start your letting-go journey to loosen old patterns and allow them to fall away, try taking these steps:

- Breathe and relax. Let yourself feel love. You can conjure it by thinking of a pet, a friend, a child.
- Feel this love as you let your heart open and relax.
- Deeply inhale and exhale. Let go without trying, simply by breathing.
- See yourself outside, on a gorgeous and tranquil beach.
- Walk on this beach. Feel the light, warm breeze and hear the gentle lapping of the ocean.
- Now, see yourself walk up to a medium-size box on a table.
- Open the box and watch butterflies take flight and soar away.
- Those were your old patterns. They have gone on to a better place, where they are free.
- It is that easy.
- Breathe and feel grateful. You let go.

After a letting-go like that, so powerful and yet light as a feather, you can feel more space and freedom inside of your body and heart. You are making space for all of the wonderful intentions you will set in Chapters 3 and 4.

The more you open your heart and relax into the goodness of your being, the more effortlessly letting-go will happen for you. Take to heart how letting-go was presented above: so easy, so safe. Be that gentle with yourself.

POTENTIAL VERSUS REALITY

Have you ever met someone you can see blooming . . . soon? You can envision his potential, whether it is spiritual, emotional, or career-related. Has this potential ever entranced you? Has it inspired you to fall in love with his future self?

Occasionally we enter into relationships based on someone's potential. Sometimes that gamble pays off. Other times, reality eventually comes crashing down. For example, you might meet someone with great spiritual potential. He may have psychic abilities that are just budding. You can easily envision that flower fully bloomed and glorious. So you enter into that relationship only to find that, a year later, the spiritual bud has not bloomed; it still remains a potential.

The root of the word *potential* itself is powerful: *potent*. As a caring, loving, empathetic caretaker, it is easy to love a man with vast potential. It can be a heady aphrodisiac to see how incredible he *might* become—especially if you can help him get there. He might really need you.

It is addictive to be needed. It seems to give your life much more meaning.

Unfortunately, this is a dangerous practice and a self-defeating behavior. It falsely feeds your self-concept to be important, to be necessary for someone to reach their potential. You need to focus on yourself, bettering your own life, not caretaking a fixer-upper boyfriend.

To spot a fixer-upper man and avoid dating him is one of the best things you can do for your dating life. Instead of taking the focus off of you and putting it on Mr. Potential, you can cultivate your best self. Then you can date men who have also cultivated their best selves. Won't that be nice? A lovely, self-actualized man who is living his potential as your date. Aim for that. Settle for nothing less.

DEVELOPING DISCERNMENT

Understanding what you've actually got instead of what you could have requires discernment. Consider this table:

DISCERNING POTENTIAL FROM REALITY	
Potential	Reality
aspires to be an activist	big unemployed dreams
openhearted	overly appreciative of other women
great dad material	playful but irresponsible
balanced ambition	workaholic
thoughtful and calm	stoned and not present
handsome Adonis type	womanizer

Developing discernment takes confidence in yourself and a commitment to listen to your intuition. Self-observation also helps. Notice how you react and feel around certain people. The flutter in your chest plus a slight sense of being off balance you felt with the boyfriend who ended up being unsupportive and using drugs may be the signal to watch for next time. Use your knowledge of your emotional and physical sensations to your advantage. Choose to discern the reality of situations.

Can he become the man of your dreams? Potential made into reality requires two key ingredients: drive and willingness to grow.

DRIVE

Drive is the intention and focus to make intentions and action happen—the effort. It takes drive to move from potential (no matter how great) to reality. Discerning who has that drive and doesn't can help you in myriad ways.

In your dates, you can spot this in their relatively graceful acceptance of constructive suggestions (usually not given by you, especially in the early stages of a relationship) coupled with steps taken to make changes as needed. For example, if your date tells a story about how at work a colleague gave him some constructive criticism to make sure to always call customers back by the next day and he accepted it and put the suggestion into practice, that would be a sign that he has the drive to reach his potential. On the other hand, if he tells a story how once when his boss gave him suggestions for improvement, he spent the next week calling in sick to use up his leave time before quitting, not only did he not show graceful acceptance of constructive suggestions, he also acted in a passive-aggressive way. Not good.

When a man has drive, it is apparent pretty quickly. Does he seem confident in his ability to make things happen and shape his reality? A guy shows his confidence in tons of little ways: the way he guides you through a crowd with a gentle touch, the way he takes action when it is needed. For example, suppose he decides his car is due to be replaced. He researches cars. Decides his price range. Figures out which one or two he wants. Goes to the dealership and makes it happen. Little hemming and hawing occurs, just action preceded by appropriate thought and consideration. *That* is the type of guy you want to date.

You also need to feel confident in your ability to shape your reality. You have a much better chance of attracting a partner with this quality if you are striving to exemplify it as well!

WILLINGNESS TO GROW

A fluid and evolving view of the universe lets us accept and embrace change in our lives and ourselves. This fluid view can make the difference between potential and reality. The guy who is willing to grow wants to realize his full potential. He will work to make that happen. Discerning whether a man has this quality will help you decide whether he is someone you can grow with. How does your guy deal with change? Does he seem to roll with it well? On a date, notice how flexible your guy acts. Does he go with the flow as plans change? Does he talk about his personal growth process? The way he worked through issues with his parents or the growth that came out of a past relationship?

An impetus and openness to growth is a valuable trait in a partner. If he can feel safe when things need to change, then he can roll with life's ebbs and flows and be there for you when you need to change. He won't fear your change, growth, or evolution; he will embrace it. What a major benefit in a relationship if both people feel safe with change. Life will be less fearful and more peaceful. With your date, find out by asking and observing: Does he feel safe when things need to change? Is his reality rocked? How much? It is human to fear the unknown a little bit, but how does your date (and potential long-term partner) manage that uncertainty? Is he willing to grow and change to better himself and enhance his spiritual development? Over time, hints will show up to inform you whether your dates are proficient in this skill. Some hints will come in stories of his life that he tells. How has he grown over the years? Does he tell stories of a quiet, shy, isolated youth who faced up to those self-conscious moments and become a great friend to many? Other hints will show up in life together, when plans change, or when major family events happen. Does he deal with his emotions and open himself to change?

Potential in Your Past

Have you dated or married someone based on their potential? Who? Ask yourself these questions about each experience:

1. What attracted you to him?
2. What reality were you hoping the two of you would arrive at when this potential was realized?
3. Did that happen?

Now look at your answers. If dating a man with potential hasn't worked out for you and you'd like to avoid it in the future, how might you do that? During the dating process, ask yourself if you are looking at your date's potential or if he has manifested its reality. For example, if he talks about spirituality and nature with you does he actually meditate or belong to a journey group? Does he walk his spiritual talk? Are his words backed up by his actions? Use your discernment and see the reality of the situation and the person.

These two ingredients, drive and willingness to grow, cook up a conscious and motivated man, one who will put effort into a relationship, just like he does for himself and his life. He will also develop and expand as a person, allowing you to comfortably do the same. This guy might challenge you. He may gently call you on things sometimes. Make sure he always does this with love. Brusque guys are not usually the best partners for sensitive women. Know yourself and what is optimum for you in a partner. Ideally, a balance is best.

As spiritual women on a conscious path, you can choose a partner who is in reality a beautiful, enhancing match. When you encounter glorious potential, latent under the surface, you can honor it and respect its attractiveness, but choose a reality that is best for you.

HEALING YOUR BODY'S MEMORY OF PAST RELATIONSHIP HURTS AND TRAUMA

Once you've examined your past for clues it can give you for choosing a better future, it's time to get any leftover energy out of your body and being. It is time to move on and stop letting the past affect you.

For those who have had traumatic relationships and chosen less-than-ideal partners, this is crucial to your future happiness. Hurts can be let go. Fears can be recognized, acknowledged, and released. Sometimes after most of the emotional and mental wounds are healed, phantom pains can linger in your body long after the experience is over. To be truly open-hearted and ready for spiritual dating, you must clear these issues and energies from your body.

We all have body memories of certain situations. Here is an example: Jane used to ride horses with her Aunt Celia every summer. They bonded and had a great time during these summers in Jane's childhood and teen years. After they went riding, Aunt Celia would always make her homemade lemonade. To Jane, it was the best drink in the world. Now twenty years later, when Jane visits Aunt Celia in her assisted living community and they drink the famous homemade lemonade together, Jane's thighs feel like she was just in the saddle all day riding. Her body remembers even though it has been twenty years.

The body's memories are powerful, visceral and kinesthetic. They are deeper than any other types of memories we have. Yet we must let them go when the time is right. When we do, we can move on even more fully and live richer, healthier lives. The following two stories show you several courageous women who faced their body memories and phantom pains and came out stronger and happier.

THE PHANTOM MENACE

A client felt a localized sharp, pointed pain in the muscle and tissue next to her vagina. She was totally healthy otherwise, so the experience puzzled her. She came to my medical intuitive practice for answers. As we looked at the energy woven through the tissue, she began to unravel it. She realized that it was a phantom pain from an operation she had undergone almost twenty years earlier. She had gotten a sexually transmitted disease from a boyfriend and had to have an operation to remove lesions from her vagina. While she was under general anesthesia, that area was numbed with an injection. The phantom pains were from that injection and also the pain from that tumultuous relationship. The guy was, in her words, "a liar and a cheater."

She breathed and kept letting go of the phantom pains from that difficult relationship. Awareness of what was up, patience, and acceptance of her process were what she needed.

I asked, "What were the gifts from the relationship and the experience?" She said, "Well, love, I guess. In spite of all the lies and hardship, there was an immature experience of love. And one of those, 'Don't do this' types of things, as far as the relationship goes. And savvyness came out of it, too."

Then we looked at her fears moving forward in her newest relationship. Could she trust? Let go? Believe in someone else's authenticity? She wanted to. With diligence and self-observation, she did it. I got a letter from her recently with a lovely wedding picture enclosed. A happy and radiant bride, she glowed. She courageously trusted her new man.

A DESERT REBORN

Danica came to my practice for help with her general state of mind and happiness. She had been avoiding getting serious with any of the guys she had dated in the past several years. When I asked her why, she said bashfully that she could not get wet for anything sexual unless she was solo.

She wanted to be sexual with serious dates. She had met some men she might have liked to make love to, but out of fear and embarrassment, she disappeared, shying away from potential connection.

We processed first that if she was going to share such a deep part of herself with a man, then she needed to be comfortable enough with him to talk about what was happening for her. She said that was actually a relief and a way that she could gauge how she felt about someone. In later appointments, we worked more on the energies and experiences involved.

Six months later, she was dating someone she could talk with about the situation. He told her they had all the time in the world and he loved her as she was. Needless to say, this was encouraging.

So it was time to delve deeper. I asked her about her past relationships and dating experiences. There were only two, and one in particular was related to what she was processing. She finally opened up about Toby. He was a long-term guy in and out of her life for years. Sometimes he showered her with affection and compliments. Then he would disappear for weeks, coming back drunk at night, wanting to see her. Those nights he would demean her when they were having sex, telling her terrible things about how her body looked or how low and worthless she was. She said she just chalked it up to drunken sex talk for years. And the good days would make up for those disrespectful nights.

One day Toby asked her to marry him—without a ring, but with what she convinced herself was an honest sentiment. She said yes and that night they tried to make love. She was dry as a bone. Nothing at all. Sex hurt so intensely that she pushed him off. He wanted to keep going anyway but she asserted herself, said no, and threw his clothes in the hall and said she never wanted to see him again. She finally snapped. Soon after she moved to another part of town so he would stop coming to her door drunk.

And that was it for her. No serious men for three years. She was ready to pick up the pieces and reassemble her body and self-concept. She said she hated herself for putting up with him. She was deeply ashamed. No wonder she couldn't relax and feel good about sex! Lots of talking about loving herself and accepting herself ensued. Then we got to the energy held in her body. A sandpaper-like energy rash was gathered around her reproductive organs and center. As together we moved the energy out and into the Earth for recycling, her uterus began gently contracting. During this healing energy experience, she was instructed to breathe deeply and fully into the area and say, "I am beautiful. I am worthy. I am loved by all life. I love myself. I love myself. I love myself. I love my body and its radiant creative and sexual center."

She left saying she felt lighter. She told me the next time that she had several dreams about letting go, some specifically about Toby and some more symbolic. A few weeks later she was ready to try intercourse with her new love. And it was lovely, honoring and really pleasurable for them both. All was well. She says sometimes things still come up but she feels loved and safe with her boyfriend and, in her words, they face it together.

HOW TO MOVE STAGNANT AND PHANTOM ENERGY

So, you've examined your patterns and learned from your choices. What do you do with the energy left behind in your body? How do you get rid of the emotions, fears, and insecurities? Eject the phantom energies and fully inhabit your body!

- Move. Exercise, dance, run, walk fast, and think of the stored energy in the body from past relationships. Move the energy or chi. Let it be easy and fun. Call up the feelings associated with the relationship—anger, fear, betrayal, sadness—and then move them out. Use deep breathing to do this while physically moving. As the feelings come to the surface, see them flow into the Earth to be recycled by the giant iron crystal at her center. They will be turned back into pure white light there and released to the universe as an offering.

- Make a list of everything you fear may happen in a future or current healthy relationship. Now, with the list in hand, state each fear aloud individually. For each one, tune in. If the fear was located in your body, where would it be? Where do you feel it? (Sometimes it helps to place your hands on your abdomen and close your eyes.) Make a note on your list of where each fear feels most active in your body.

  Breathe into each body area and state, "I let go of the fear of _____." Keep breathing and repeating the statement gently until you feel the fear-energy soften and dissolve. Keep the list for awhile. You may need to do this letting-go exercise more than once.

- Brainstorm all of the feelings you may be holding about your past relationships, hookups, flirtations—all of your

sexual and intimate experiences. Start by intellectually list-
ing what your emotions might be or have been.

- Next, go into your heart, in the center of your chest. Feel
  what is present there. Simply notice. Add any new emotions you find to the brainstormed ones.

- Choose one feeling you would like to let go of. Create a
  representation of it. Draw a picture of it. Write it on a slip
  of paper. Create a clay sculpture of it.

- How could you symbolically let go of the representation?
  Burn the paper safely. Squish the clay into a ball. While
  doing this, let yourself feel the feeling wash through you
  and gently drain out. If it is not fully draining, try again
  another day. Letting go of emotions is not a process that can
  be rushed. The heart has its own timing.

DISCONNECT FROM PAST DATES AND PARTNERS

A clear and clean energy body fosters optimum health and happiness. Your energy body is the area around and throughout your
physical body. It is made of electromagnetic energy, spiritual
energy, emotional energy, mental energy, and your vital life force.
It is what defines your personal space. Some people call it your
aura.

Sometimes our energy or vital life force can get clouded or
bogged down by our physical and emotional contact with other
people. Disconnecting from past dates and partners is an easy
way to feel lighter and brighter. Often it is necessary to dissolve
energetic and emotional ties to past loves to make space for new
love to come into our lives. Each relationship is an elaborate
and complex dance of energetic exchange. When we stop dating
someone and start being platonic friends, some of the old energy

pathways that were part of our romantic relationship can remain. For a short time this can help people let go of each other by degrees. For more than a few months, though, it is unhealthy. It keeps us from fully moving on and having the ability to eventually create new, healthy romantic connections. Exes—husbands, wives, boyfriends, girlfriends, lovers, even one-night stands—must be in their proper and healthy place for future relationships to function properly. Otherwise, issues crop up. Sometimes they are issues of emotional connection that detract from the current romantic relationship. Sometimes they are issues of one ex-partner wanting to control the other, creating a three-person dynamic in a relationship that should only have the two current lovers actively participating. Sometimes old partners have heavy vibrations that are not positive for us and when we let the old ties go, the heavy energy leaves our lives.

Disconnect from all past sexual partners' energies for all time. Do this by stating the following aloud with intention: "I now disconnect from _____ (list all partners' names or say "all of my dates and sexual partners") for all time in all dimensions, all interdimensions, and all realities as needed for my highest good and the highest good of all life. I release all energies associated with these sexual relationships from my life and being in the spirit of gratitude and ask that they be released from my focus for all time. It is done."

HEALING YOUR HEART

Our hearts are both the most delicate and most resilient parts of us. When we read about "triumphs of the human spirit," it is our hearts that are starring in those dramas—and our hearts' strings that are stirred by witnessing them. How do we heal an emotional organ?

There is not a prescription or drug to provide a quick fix. Instead, we have to go a different route. That route is *joy*.

Trusting Archangels

Healing hearts is a specialty of a group of spirit beings known to some as the Archangels. For the purpose of this book, this word and these beings have no religious significance. The Archangels are simply beings who have pledged a portion of their attention, for their entire lives, to helping humans and the Earth. In a way, they are a part of us.

Archangels specialize in joy for healing. They can help you raise your spirits and mend a broken heart. They can heal your emotional energy body and your precious, tender heart. Ask them to let your heart be healed.

Healing our hearts with joy takes time. It is sometimes the process of our dog snuggling us after a breakup, night after night. Or the conscious effort we make each day to love ourselves. With a belief in something greater—Spirit, the Divine, the Goddess, God, the Source—we can ask for help. We can say, "I open to joy and unconditional divine love to fill my heart and melt my sadness. It is done."

MAKE TIME FOR JOY

Making time to experience joy is the single most important thing you can do to heal your heart. Heart healing is an alchemical art of sorts. It uses the most magical powers in the universe. Delve into your heart with courage! You are supported.

You can make time for joy in a conscious manner. Schedule "joy time" each day, even if for only five minutes. That could be when you take a walk in the sun among flowers in the park on your lunch hour. It could be making a commitment to yourself that each day you will do something joyful whether it is singing your favorite power anthem in the car while driving or setting a morning intention each day about the joy you will let in and draw to you. However it works for you, daily joy will improve your life manyfold.

The Violet Flame Energy Cleanse

Cleanse your energy field using the following meditation on the Violet Flame. The Violet Flame is a ray of cleansing energy held by all of the amethyst minerals in the crust of the Earth. It is spectacularly effective in clearing your auric field, the area of energy around and throughout your physical body, also known as your personal space.

Cleansing your energy body will help you "broadcast" who you are in a clearer, more resonant manner. That way, the right dates will be able to spot you quickly and easily. And in the tradition of science and energy, the most basic principle applies: Like attracts like. Of course, you would like a clear and clean guy to date, so in turn you must be putting out this clear, clean vibe so he will innately want to date you. Give it a try!

1. State aloud, "With gratitude, I now call forth the Violet Flame of Ascension to cleanse my physical and energetic bodies and auric field."
2. Envision a column of purple fire coming up through the Earth below you. Next, see it rise up through and around you. Feel it moving through your being and burning away all that does not serve you. Breathe deeply. Each breath draws the Violet Flame up through you.

3. Stay focused on the purple flame as it moves through your body and the space around your body. Be thorough and allow it to clear every cell of your being. Envision your body and a sphere stretching about five feet out all around you completely engulfed in the violet cleansing fire.

4. When that feels complete, envision a column of pure, white light above you and watch that column descend around and through you. Feel it fill up everywhere that the Violet Flame cleansed. Again, be thorough and take your time infusing each cell with white light.

Important Note: When using The Violet Flame you must follow up with white light. It is crucial to fill the cleared areas with white light and not leave them open.

HEART HEALING USING THE POWER OF JOY

Joy is the most healing and highly vibrational energy in the known universe. When you consciously use that power for healing your heart, miracles happen! Let your heart heal now as you delve into healing through joy.

- Visualize a ball of golden light before you. Say the word yes aloud to this ball three times and tell the ball it is joy, also three times.

- Ask this ball to expand and encompass the entire room you are in and, if you would like, your entire house and yard. You can do this wherever you are, even in the local coffee shop.

- Place your attention on your heart, on the center of your chest.

- Call forth ultimate power by saying aloud, "I call forth all of the magnetic resonance particles in the universe that love joy! Whoo hoo! I am about to throw the best joy party you have ever seen, please help me. This party is in my heart and entire emotional body. Everyone meet there in 5, 4, 3, 2, 1—now!"
- Clap your hands together vigorously three times (which creates a paradigm shift). See, feel, and know the entirety of the joy ball as it condenses into the area selected with a whoosh.
- Sing or hum the most joyful songs, sounds, and tones. Allow these to spontaneously bubble out of you. If that isn't quite happening, then fake it till you make it. Sing something, even if it is simply "My heart is healing, my heart is healing."
- When you have sung your heart out (you are the entertainment for the joy party!), wind it down a bit vocally but keep the joyful feeling and let it become a peaceful joy. Feel the joyful energy particles at the party inside of you begin to sway in unison, as if they are holding hands by candlelight in peaceful communion, humming for peace, honoring joy.
- Lie down for at least thirty minutes and feel yourself in the center of a multitiered circle of the humming, swaying energy particles. Drift off to sleep if you can.
- You will feel when the party is complete. The joy and healing will remain for all time.
- Use this process as often as you would like and always allow the rest period after for the best results.
- Thank the Archangels for this. They threw the party.

OPENING TO LOVE

Feelings are like water. Even years after an overwhelming flood there is still damage. Postcleanup, all seems well, but an echo remains. Opening to love again after a flood of heartbreak is a bit like picking up the pieces of a flooded town. First you process the pain and trauma. Next you rebuild and learn from the mistakes. Then it is time to move on. Or so society would tell you. But what do you do when it is hard to move on? What do you do when the flood is still echoing?

All you need ask of yourself is small steps: the choice to smile at a passerby who smiles at you. A willingness to feel love from family members in a deeper, more real way. Considering the possibility that you might like to date again. These are great first steps when you are ready and there is truly no rush.

Here is the fact that can let you open again: You have *great* instincts. You are going to use this book and identify all of your heart's red flags; you are going to demystify dating in a new way. You are going to learn about chemical smells and sexual tension and preventing energy predators. You are now armed with the information you need from within you, supplemented with the book in your hands. You are ready. You can trust your instincts. You have chosen to be conscious and so you are. It is that easy. Small steps as you learn about spiritual dating will keep you comfortable.

Being open to love makes your body more healthy and raises your emotional satisfaction level. A heart and being open to love is a powerful, radiant force. Opening to love has to do with opening to deeply, truly loving yourself. That comes first. Then, calmly, unhurriedly, you can allow life to provide you with date or a partner at the perfect time. There is no rush when you are filled with universal and self-love. Can you allow yourself to be filled by life, by spirit, by friends, by family? Can you receive just the best love energy from everything and let the rest fall away? Yes, you can.

Simply ask and life will deliver: "Please fill me with universal life force and deep, unwavering, unconditional love for myself and all life. Help me soften and open to love and bring me only the best, most well-intentioned love for my highest good. Thank you so much. I am grateful. It is done."

As you open to love, you can begin the process of defining your intentions for your dating life. In the next chapter, you will learn about further strengthening yourself and becoming a magnetic force of nature. Your healing heart can do this with ease and gentleness. You are ready. Take the next step and intend what you want.

Part Two

Define Your Intention

In Part 2, it is time to figure out who you are in an even more complete way. This knowledge will help you define your intentions about what you want to create in your dating life. Intentions are "wishes" on which you are applying your focus to turn into reality. If you have an intention to meet a dog-loving, kind man through an online dating platform, you formulate that intention in your mind and heart. Then you create an online dating profile, which is a deliberate step toward your making your intention to meet this man a reality. Then you interact with potential men over the online dating platform to determine if they fit your dog-loving, kind criteria. Eventually, you find that man by combining your deliberate actions with a sense of allowing and trusting that he is out there.

In this part, you'll learn how to create intentions that strengthen you. The stronger and more solid you are in yourself, the more attractive you are to spiritual men who are also solid and strong. You can make the most of your inner strength and be true to yourself while on the dating scene. You'll also learn about authenticity—what it is and why you should strive toward it—and you'll also spend some time realizing what you want in a partner, a date, a friend. How do you envision your love life? What are your needs? We have a lot to do. Let's get started!

Chapter Three
Strengthening Yourself

Have you ever been out on a date and felt awkward, uncomfortable, or out of place? Have you ever come home from a bad date and felt that the evening wasn't exactly what you expected it to be because you weren't smart enough, funny enough, pretty enough? In order to turn a date into a second date and a second date into a relationship, you need to cultivate your inner strength.

What is inner strength? It is the invisible but very real fortitude inside of you. It is an internal power source made of feeling that you can count on yourself. Your inner strength is your faith in your own reliability. It isn't measurable but it is very real. It is what gets you through tough times and keeps your outlook positive. Your inner strength sustains you. It is your spiritual and emotional fuel.

Your inner strength also magnifies your intentions because it makes them stronger. It amplifies your power so your intentions come out of you more clearly and with more force behind them. In this chapter, you'll learn how to bulk up your own inner strength and how to use it to your best advantage to realize your dating intentions.

DAZZLE YOUR DATES

Some people are dazzling, charismatic, attractive. They pull you in; they're magnetic. That's the kind of person you want to be when you're searching for the perfect guy. Now don't misunderstand the idea here. You don't have to become someone different just to land a guy; you just have to be the best you possible. Not sure how to put your best foot forward? Well, in their highest expression these dazzling people have the following five traits that you should strive to exude:

- They love themselves and they know who they are.
- They are confident.
- They are authentic—they are just themselves.
- They own their sexuality and consciously direct their sexual energy.
- They are magnetic.

You may not realize it now, but you already hold the key to becoming one of these dazzling people. All you have to do is embrace your inner strength and learn to love yourself for who you really are. To make it easy, each of these dazzling qualities is broken down throughout the rest of the chapter.

SELF-LOVE IS GORGEOUS

When it comes right down to it, there is nothing more attractive than self-love. If your intention is to attract a man who loves himself in a healthy way, than you have to be rooted in love for yourself, too. You have to demonstrate the self-love that you seek in a partner. Your healthy love for yourself is sexy! It is hot, and sweet, and kind—all the things a spiritual man wants in a partner.

If you're having trouble finding self-love, remember that you don't have to be perfect. We all make mistakes and part of loving yourself is accepting that and being able to move on from it. Don't live in the past because you can't change it. Instead, accept yourself and love yourself because you exist. You are here on Earth in a body and your heart beats, you have feelings, your mind is alive. You are perfect because of your imperfections. You are learning, growing, changing. You are loved by life, by spirit, by existence. It is not an accident that you are here. Love yourself for that. You are important.

TREAT YOURSELF

Cultivate self-love by showing yourself how special you are. Think of the ways you would treat a treasured lover. How would you spoil that person? How would you like to be showered with love by your true love? Do that for yourself! Send or get yourself a bouquet of your favorite flowers, make your favorite meal and eat it by candlelight followed by a luxurious bubble bath, hug yourself when you get home in the evening in joy that you get to spend time with yourself, take yourself for a beach day of fun complete with your favorite sand toys and beach treats. Can you commit to doing at least one of your self-love expressions per day for yourself as a real-world demonstration of how you love yourself?

JEN TAKES HERSELF ON A SEXY DATE

Jen was feeling low. She was bereft after her best friend moved away three months after her boyfriend did the same. She felt lonely and wanted to connect with new friends and especially new, high-quality guys.

She realized she needed to demonstrate to herself her deep love for herself. This would help her feel less lonely and much more loved. It would fill her up. She planned a great weekend for herself. Friday night she stayed in and made her favorite dinner, organic chicken parmesan with endive and arugula salad. She watched two of her favorite romantic, uplifting movies, *Practical Magic* and *Miss Congeniality*. Then she went to bed on her freshly made and lavender-scented bed.

Saturday morning she awoke recharged and rested. She had a leisurely morning reading and sipping tea and then took a fun walk in the park. Late that afternoon, she took a decadent bubble bath. She moisturized and pampered every inch of her body. Then she got dressed in her new turquoise minidress and favorite strappy heels and took herself to a fabulous dinner at her favorite restaurant. She ate and enjoyed people watching, letting herself feel comfortable in her aloneness.

As she finished her meal and walked through the bar, she was approached by a man. He asked her, "You are the most confident, sexiest woman I have seen in a long time. I know it is a long shot, but will you have dinner with me?"

She looked at him and paused as she thought of what to say. He took it as a fumble on his part and said, flustered, "I did this in the wrong order. I'm Ken. What's your name?"

They proceeded to talk for another hour or so. In the end, she did agree to a date with Ken and they had a lovely time together the following weekend and for many weekends after.

Even as she dated Ken, Jen still remembered it was her self-love that got her through everything and she cultivated it in a healthy way, always honoring who she was and what she wanted out of life.

CONFIDENCE IS SEXY

You know those confident women who walk down the street, seemingly with a sassy, sexy theme song playing in the background? What is their secret? Why are they so alluring? It all comes back to confidence. Those women have got it and they know it. It really isn't about how they look; it is how they feel that shines through. When you feel confident, you take more chances. You make things happen. You know you can handle life's ups and downs. This is especially important when you're dating.

Keep It Confident

What are your positive traits? What are you good at? What are you proud of about yourself? List twenty great things about yourself.

If you're having trouble finding your confidence, keep in mind that confidence comes from within. It is an internal, pervasive feeling of rightness. You are "right." You are perfect as you are. You accepted yourself and you know you are in the right place, as the right person, and you have faith in that rightness. To help boost your confidence throughout your day-to-day life try noticing these things:

- Notice when you smile at a stranger.
- Notice when you help another person.
- Notice when you compliment someone else and when you are complimented.
- Notice the resilience with which you walk through your world.
- Notice yourself. Pay attention to who you are and how wonderful that is.

All of the above examples illustrate your confidence in yourself. You take the risk of smiling at a stranger, possibly brightening their day and yours. There is a slight risk of rejection in the form of not being smiled at in response. But you have the confidence to go for it anyway. Imagine how that confidence could help you get a date!

Why is confidence so important when you're out there looking for your spiritual mate? For one, your feelings of confidence tell you that you are worthy. You are deserving of a great guy who loves you and treats you well. You deserve a happy life.

Your confidence makes you attractive to potential dates. It showcases your strengths and shines through your being, drawing people to you. You make it easy to see how wonderful you are when you already know this. Spiritual, emotionally healthy men want to date you when you are confident. It lets them see that you are their equal—that even though you each have strengths and weaknesses, you can meet each other on a level playing field. You are a good match for a great man when you are confident in yourself.

BOOST CONFIDENCE

You can also boost your confidence by kicking your insecurities to the curb. Sometimes our insecurities can get in the way of our feeling confident and powerful—and they leave us feeling that we don't deserve a great guy, or that we are not worthy of goodness in our lives. Get those insecurities out in the open right now by doing the following exercise.

SHOW INSECURITIES YOUR INTENTION

To banish your insecurities you must first realize what they are.

1. On a piece of notebook paper, make a list of your insecurities, leaving some space to make notes next to each one.

   • Go back through your list. For each insecurity ask yourself the following questions:

      • Is the insecurity rooted in a fear? If so, what are you afraid could happen?
      • Where did the insecurity come from? Did someone tell you this about yourself? Where might you have gotten this message and when?

- Note your thoughts next to each insecurity.
- Now that you have identified some of the fears that block your growth and progress, take a look at each insecurity on your list and, for each one, state aloud, "I now release _____ (example: my fear of not being smart enough) to be transformed back into neutral energy. I am done with it and, although grateful for any past blessings it bestowed, I now part ways with this fear or insecurity for all time. I choose joy and light to replace it. It is done."
- Now breathe deeply with your eyes closed and feel like you are a hot air balloon floating higher and higher. Let go and become lighter.
- Now, create a positive affirmative statement for each insecurity on your list. For example, if the insecurity is "Men are not attracted to my shy personality," you would write something like "Guys I meet appreciate my kind spirit and gentle manner." Use these affirmations whenever you feel yourself slipping back into not feeling good enough. Repeat them to yourself. Post reminders around your house that say things like: *I am happy and confident. I value myself. I am perfect as I am, I accept myself. I am proud of myself. I choose to see my goodness and celebrate my achievements.*

2. By doing this you're basically retraining yourself to think positively and confidently. That is the secret of confident people. Most of the time, they think confident thoughts. It doesn't mean that they are arrogant. It means they value themselves. They see their goodness and how they enhance their world. They celebrate their achievements.

YOUR AUTHENTIC SELF

Your authentic self is your true being, who you really are. It is who you are deep within, in all of your complex glory. Your authentic self is also your spiritual self, your inner radiance. Meeting, knowing, and eventually embodying your authentic self is crucial to being a spiritual dater. You must know yourself. You must be yourself with confidence when you date your true love. Your real partner, the right person, must be authentically himself, too. You need to fall in love with each other's reality, each other's authentic selves.

If you've been shoving your authentic self to the background lately, give her a break and let her out. You don't have to pretend to be someone you're not—and you're not going to find the man of your dreams if you do! Speak your true mind a bit more. Laugh when you think something is funny. Dress the way you want to dress. Aligning with your authentic self strengthens you in so many ways. It lets your true self shine through. That self is who your soul mates, friends, and partners will be attracted to. That is who they will see and love.

When you start to showcase who you really are, you also send your true self the message that she is loved and right. This is *so* crucial to your emotional health. Too many women doubt themselves because they have internalized the thought that something about them is not right, correct, the way it should be. Doubting yourself shows up when you don't listen to your intuition. Like when you have the intuitive impulse that a man you are on a first date with is a player and push it to the side, only to see him getting the waitress's phone number as you walk back from the bathroom on your third date. We doubt what we really know. But your authentic self cannot doubt. She is truth. She knows. When you align the person you show to the world with her, you will be more sure of yourself and many of your doubts and fears will fall away. So explore your authentic self. Align with your true being. All will be well.

OWN YOUR SEXUALITY

In this case, ownership is claiming what is already yours. Owning your sexuality starts with owning your space. When you own your space, you will feel safer, more confident, and able to be your authentic self. When you own your space, no matter what skeevy guy looks at your chest or what obnoxious driver glares at you from her car, you are energetically unaffected. You are present and fill the space through and around you. When you go to a dance club, you won't invite gross guys to start grinding at you when you are just dancing with your girlfriends. You make for an attractive and self-possessed date infused with your own inner strength. Tantalizing!

Now, how would it feel to own your life? State aloud, "I own my space. I own my life. I own my body." Feel the full presence of your vital life force throughout your life. It makes things clear and clean.

Now, how would it feel to own your sexuality? Take a moment to imagine. Step into it now; state, "I own my sexuality." It is another variation of feeling present. It means you are in power in regard to the sexual use of your body, your sexual thoughts, and your sexual and sensual choices. It also means you can become more aware of your sexuality and sexual energy and where it is going.

You are a sexual being. It can't be denied. That energy is within you and it is very strong and powerful yet soft and vulnerable and everything in between. By owning your sexuality, you decide who gets to dip into that energy. Many people will want to. It is part of our cultural paradigm right now for women to invite sexually oriented interaction. You own your sexuality so you can consciously direct any of that power toward a potential suitor. You choose if you let a drop of sexual energy seep out as you lock eyes with a cute guy on the street. That level of confidence and self-assurance means that if you do direct your sexual energy at a date, it is potent. He feels it to his toes and it might only be from a smoldering look across the table at dinner. Your sexuality is even more powerful when consciously directed and not randomly leaking. When you are deliberate with your sexual energy, the men you grace with it feel extra privileged.

By owning and being conscious of your sexual energy, you will be able to leak less of that power unconsciously and use it to your benefit and for your best health.

HARNESSING THE POWER OF YOUR OWN SEXUAL ENERGY

You have an amazing reservoir of power within you, your sexual energy. It is boundless. It encompasses your full being. You are the source of this energy. You are, in essence, divine.

Part of this power stems from your womb. It is your creative center. You create life from it. You create beauty from it in so many forms: kind words, works of art, math equations, inventions, innovations, acts of love, new dance moves, and endless others.

Your sexual energy stems from this place and from your heart center. The creative energy of your womb combined with the love energy of your heart make a powerful force that can enliven and enhance your life. This energy can also be harnessed for the general betterment of the planet, to infuse Earth with love and peace, and to better your life.

CONNECT WITH YOUR CREATIVE SEXUAL ENERGY

To harness the power of your creative sexual energy, practice the following activity.

1. Bring your attention to your womb area.

   - Place your hands there and affirm aloud, "I love and honor my womb, my heart, and my divine creative power."
   - Breathe into the area and evoke feelings of self-love. Think about how perfect you are, simply because you exist. Feel love flowing up from the Earth below you up through your body into your womb.
   - Now think of something wholly loving you would like to use the power of your womb to create. It will only work if it is for the highest good of all life and helps all and harms none.
   - Breathe and let the power of your womb and heart expand with more feelings of self-love.
   - When your breathing reaches a crescendo or climax think of your intention and let the energy release like golden fireworks from your center. Whatever energy is not used for your intention will be returned to your body for healing and enlivenment.

2. You can do this activity while making love to yourself once you have practiced it and feel proficient with the technique. Combined with the energetic buildup of self-lovemaking the loving power gathered will be great.

USING AFFIRMATIONS

Another way to strengthen your feminine power is through affirmations. Try saying these aloud and posting your favorites around the house:

- "I am feminine strength and softness."
- "I am the goddess. All acts of love and pleasure affirm my light."
- "I am the creative principle, forever unfolding."
- "I am a force of peace and light and my body is infused with this force."
- "I am my Higher Self."
- "I am power and passion and I enhance all life simply by being me."

You can create your own affirmative statements, too. Create one now!

Your sexuality is a key component of your dating self. You need to own your sexuality and your space to really feel the full scope of your desire, or not, for a date. Embody your infinite womanly power. It is bootylicious!

EXERCISE YOUR MAGNETISM

Magnetism. It makes everything happen. We attract energy, life situations, and people to ourselves. Sometimes we are not aware of the way we unconsciously shape our lives through what we attract. That is why awareness is so important.

In dating, magnetism attracts our suitors and compels them to ask us out or motivates us to ask them out. We magnetize the type of men we set our intentions upon. If we haven't yet set any intentions, then we magnetize men based on old data such as similarity to other men in our lives or by reenacting old patterns. That is why we are setting clear intentions about our dating lives in this book, so that we can set new patterns.

Your magnetism is made up of your charisma, your sexuality, your thoughts, your feelings, your energy body, your mind power, your intention, and your focus. Your authentic self is the strongest part of your magnetism. If you are not aligned with it, your magnet is not as strong. So, the more you embody your authentic self, the better your life can be. Your magnet will be strong and attract your heart's desire. For some, that can translate into the dates you crave and the partner you know is out there somewhere.

Enhance and Activate Your Magnetism

1. Focus on your power center. Where do you feel it? Your navel? Belly? Heart center? Solar plexus?
2. Feel the energy radiating from there.
3. Notice a large sphere at the center of that energy. It is spinning, revolving.
4. Increase the speed with which that sphere revolves. State, "Center speed increase and activate."
5. Feel even more power radiating from that center as it speeds up.
6. Now state, "I activate and enhance my charisma energy as needed for my highest good. I am fully safe and secure within my enhanced charismatic life."

Your magnetism is fueled by your power center. It is intimately intertwined with your sexuality. Your magnetism is not always sexual, though. It is mostly neutral energy—sheer power. Charisma is intertwined with your magnetic self. Your charisma is the force that flows from your center and attracts what you want. It can be harnessed to enhance your life. A charismatic person makes you feel at once included and at the same time somewhat in awe.

The other component of your magnetism is boundaries—your ability to repel what you don't want while attracting what you do want. Consciousness of your magnetism and awareness of your power help set your boundaries for your best life experience. You can activate your boundary energy very simply.

Just state, "I activate my magnetic boundaries and power to repel what does not serve me, now. It is done."

Chapter Four
Put in Your Sales Order

Now that you have looked at who you are, it's time to determine what you want. In this chapter, you will put in your sales order for everything you want in your life—your career, the general circumstances of your life, and especially your love life. By defining what you want in your life, you can use your innate magnetism to attract it. Your innate magnetism is the powerful pull of your authentic self that draws people and situations to you. Your intention is magnified by your magnetism. That certainly goes for guys, dating, and romance.

Dating can be an exercise in magnetic attraction. You can meet soul mates and heart friends by defining what you are looking for and desire in a relationship and then attracting it through creating a Love Life Roadmap. You'll find out how to create your Roadmap later in this chapter.

Think of it: You put in your sales order and then you follow your Love Life Roadmap to your ultimate destination—while thoroughly enjoying the journey there. Let's get started!

EMBRACE YOUR SACRED FUTURE

Sacredness means you are heavenly in a totally nonreligious way. You are made of sacred beauty. This is a fact. Once you integrate that truth into the very fiber of your being, self-love will be natural and easy. Loving yourself is required for authentic relationships. It is required to be a spiritual dater. That is why it is the first step in creating your Love Life Roadmap. With your sacredness confirmed within you, you can create a life that honors and supports you. Want that for yourself! Strive for it! Aspire to it! And mostly, just do it.

As you become more secure in the knowledge that you are sacred, you can create a new future, one that is joyful and expansive, one that honors your sacredness, your quirks, your wants and needs. You can create a future that accepts you for who you are and who you aspire to be.

DEFINE YOUR SACRED FUTURE

Keeping in mind your sacred essence, the truth that you are divine and worthy of love and respect, ask yourself some questions about the future.

- Where do you see yourself and how are you living in one year?
- What is the prevalent feeling of your life?
- How are you spending your time?
- Are you happy in your career?
- Where are you living? What is it like?
- How about your love life?
- How does your confirmation of your sacredness shape your entire life?

Now ask yourself some questions about where you see yourself in five years, still keeping your sacred essence in mind.

- What will your sacred life look like in five years?
- How much great change will you have integrated?

- What will your career, living situation, love life look like then?
- What will your life be like? Or more importantly, what would you like it to be like?
- How will that be different from your current reality?

PLAN YOUR SACRED FUTURE

Now that you have an idea of what you'd like your future to look like, what steps do you need to take to get to that new place in the future? Ask yourself a few questions:

- How can you take your life to its most optimum, sacred, loving place?
- How can you engage with your life and become more joyful, happier, because you are so worth it?

Small steps applied over time are fine.

Now, think about some changes you need to make to get to where you would truly like to be.

- Do you need to make a career change? What would be your dream career?
- Do you need to live somewhere else? A better dwelling, a different climate?
- How can you move toward that?

Finally, look at your love life.

- Do you want to rehab your love life?
- What feelings do you want to feel as a result of your dating and relationship life?

- What do you want to be doing in regard to your love life?
- Spending your time how?

JENNY'S SACRED JOURNEY

Here is an example of a woman who decided she was ready to create a life worthy of her sacredness. In 1999, Jenny realized her sacredness completely. From that time forward, she systematically and methodically began making over her life. She longed to work with people in a dynamic setting and wanted to move to a hot, dry climate after years of cold, wet Michigan winters. She got her wish! She moved to Las Vegas in 2000 to work as a manager in a lively casino.

Over the next few years, she created a beautiful home that reflected her taste. She loved decorating and had a penchant for it. She realized she wanted to explore that as an additional career path. The opportunity arose and she redecorated one of the ballrooms in the hotel where she worked. Then she was asked to redo the lobby. Soon she was the staff image-and-decorating consultant for the entire hotel and casino.

Next, she identified the type of partner she wanted: caring, gentle, artistic, yet masculine and chivalrous. She dated with this ideal in mind. She took it slowly and was deliberate and conscious about whom she dated. In 2002, she met Steve and he fit with her life in a way that felt good and natural. They are still together, happy and fulfilled in their lives.

HONOR YOUR SACREDNESS

Now that you have a better understanding of how honoring your sacredness can play out in your life, it's time to ask a few more questions.

1. Are there situations or parts of your life at the present time that are incongruent with your sacredness?
2. Do you have a lover who is demeaning or unkind, or doesn't see how sacred you and he are?
3. Do you have to go against what you think is right to keep your job?
4. Do you lie to people in your life?
5. Do you passively allow a family member to put you down?

Now, on a separate piece of paper, list the ways your life is incongruous with your sacredness. Then go back over your list and write one or more steps to change that item into something that honors your sacredness and the sacredness of all life.

For the above examples, jettison the lover who demeans you. Find a job where you feel you are living with integrity. Make a commitment to be truthful and honor your word. Tell the family member verbally or in a letter that you will no longer accept the putdowns. Each time they happen after that, leave the situation. Find the simple solutions to your complex problems!

KNOW WHAT YOU WANT

Know what you want. If only it were that easy, right? You may have thought you just wanted a sensitive guy, then you date a needy sap and suddenly you crave a sports-obsessed lumberjack. After dating a melancholy stoner, you may think you want a guy who will go out and have fun with you, only to find that after the tenth town parade or firemen's benefit pancake breakfast, you just kind of want to veg out in pajamas for the next month.

These are cases of missing the big picture of your emotional and companionship needs. The problem with the needy sap and Mr.

Joiner was not their activities, it was your lack of knowledge of *yourself*. What you're really looking for goes beyond the way someone looks or their hobbies; it is who they are on a deeper level.

To know what you want, you need to know yourself. If you know who you are, you can identify who would be compatible with you. You can also define how you want to live and spend your time and what kind of partner you want to be a part of that.

Start by looking at your close friendships. You may think understanding your emotional and companionship needs requires you to meditate on your personality and your past experiences, but this self-awareness can actually come through looking at the relationships you currently have. What do you value in each of those close friendships? The "say anything that comes to mind" vibe? The way you are emotionally similar and really understand each other? The kindness and the loving way your friend treats you? The cruise-director friend who always plans a fun night for everyone? The hip and up-to-the-minute friend who knows what is happening in your city? The friend who is the best counselor and is always on your side? The friend who loves hanging out with your family like you do?

List the most important of your friends' great qualities here.

1. _____
2. _____
3. _____
4. _____
5. _____

To consider a guy for a first date, which of these qualities must he have?

1. _____

2. _____

3. _____

In a long-term romantic partner, which of these qualities are necessary?

1. _____

2. _____

3. _____

Keep in mind these great qualities your friends have. Notice who among your potential dates has them. Knowing what you want just requires a bit of extra self-awareness.

Now ask yourself a question and do not censor your answer. Just say aloud the first thing that comes to mind. Ready? Ask, "What do I want?" Write it down.

1. _____

What is your answer about? Love life? Work life? Accomplishing something? Whatever it is, that is forefront in your mind. It's what you want. Simple, yes. But also important. It tells you where you are—if your head is in the dating game or if your work or children or whatever are ahead of your love life. No answer is good or bad. But if your career is forefront, then one thing you want in a dating relationship is obviously the time and space to focus on your career goals.

If your answer was that you want your children to be happy and well cared for, then of course any dating or long-term partners for you must be an enhancement not only to your happiness but your kids' happiness. In a way, these are obvious things, but sometimes pheromones, desire, or need for companionship give us temporary amnesia about what we want.

Now, ask yourself, again writing down your first response: "What *else* do I want?" Remember it. It's important.

1. _____

The "what else" answer is usually something like peaceful living, fun, and passion—qualities of experience that you crave. These are telling, too. They should come from your deeper desires, not just in response to your last date or relationship gone bad.

Qualities and types of experience you crave tell you more about your heart's desire, what you want to be doing, and how you want to feel: Safe. Tranquil. Electrified. Your inner state of mind and emotional state start to reveal themselves when you ask what else you want. Notice this about yourself. Delve into yourself.

Next, ask yourself, "What do I crave emotionally?" Once again, make a note of it.

1. _____

Some answers might be: validation, affection, love, peacefulness, emotional security, happiness, and joy. Sometimes, upon reflection, the answer to this question points to childhood wounds or unmet needs. You need to be aware of these before embarking on a new relationship. If you know that you are craving something emotionally, then you can look at:

1. When that unmet need originated and why.
2. How you can fill it on your own.

Meanings of Emotional Cravings

Sometimes, our emotional cravings are highlighted by the material things and foods we crave.

- For example, it is relatively common knowledge that a chocolate craving from an emotional place means we crave love and rich, decadent sweetness in our emotional lives.
- Wanting to shop might mean we want to experience the powerful hit of feel-good chemicals we get when we feel that we got a good deal or to demonstrate to ourselves that we are worthy of extravagance.
- If we crave in an emotional way to hear a particular song on the radio, it can mean that song makes us feel a certain way and we want to experience that feeling. Music evokes emotions.
- A craving for a cup of chamomile tea might signify a need for comfort and nurturing.

These cravings are not necessarily destructive if they are moderate; they tell us a bit about what is missing for our optimum emotional health. What does your emotional craving(s) say about you?

Not all emotional cravings show up as food or material things that you long for. Some are straightforward and obvious.

For example, craving peace might mean that your life is full and maybe a bit hectic. You would do well with a partner who is calm and helpful in creating peace and calmness in your home and therefore your internal environment as well.

- Craving passion might mean that you need to be shaken up and sensually enticed. A man who voluptuously feeds you juicy fruits and challenges your mind could fill your need for spice.
- Craving joy might mean you are feeling depressive or melancholy and you need lots of joy in your day-to-day life. A partner who

values joyful experiences and has a joyful emotional baseline could be a good and enhancing partner for you.

- Craving love could mean that you feel underappreciated or lonely. A loving man who is affectionate and likes to cuddle may bring you comfort. In this case, self-love will also fill your needs and a snuggly pet can also become a trusted friend.

If you know what you're missing and what you want, you will be more likely to find the right person to date. And knowing what you want helps you find other ways to fill your emotional needs. Self-love means providing all the love you crave for yourself and treating yourself like a treasured lover. In the spirit of self-love, if you realize you like to cuddle, maybe you can provide a snuggly pet for yourself and he or she can become a trusted friend!

Then you won't haul that heavy baggage into your next relationship. If you are craving validation, you might notice that your parents were very sparing with praise and you can decide to make a commitment to honor your accomplishments and praise yourself on a daily basis. You might commit to five praiseful sentences to yourself each day. If you are craving love and affection, you might notice how your first romantic relationship lacked it and look back further to if you had emotionally demonstrative parents. How could you provide that for yourself? Maybe you could hug yourself each morning and say aloud, "I love you, _____ (insert your first name here)." You need to know your emotional baseline and where you are coming from with your emotional needs. In Chapter 2, we covered more about how to process the past. You can go back and skim that again to help you with this exercise. Journal about how your emotional cravings may have started, how they have previously motivated your behavior, and how you can fill them yourself. Write in a free-flowing way. Make drawings and charts or tic-tac-toe-like tables. Free-associate words to get your right brain and left brain working together. You can relax and meditate prior to doing this, too, and set an intention to move old patterns, emotions, and energy. You can write a few sentences or many pages about this. Your cravings show you a lot of information. They indicate your emotional state. That is important to understand as you embark on spiritual dating.

YOUR IDEAL PARTNER'S MOST IMPORTANT QUALITIES

Starting to think about what you like in a partner and how you could enhance each other is an important step on the path of defining your intention and then, in perfect timing, manifesting your man. Rate the following qualities in a partner from most to least important by numbering them 1 to 45:

_____ attractive

_____ nature enthusiast

_____ sexy

_____ funny

_____ high sex drive

_____ ambitious

_____ good listener

_____ kind

_____ wants a family

_____ would be a good father

_____ emotionally healthy

_____ self-aware

_____ spiritual

_____ cheerful

_____ intelligent

_____ perceptive

_____ environmentally conscious

_____ eating habits similar to yours

_____ good conversationalist

_____ social

_____ introverted

_____ calm and tranquil countenance

_____ in good physical shape

_____ flexible

_____ organized

_____ loves animals

_____ affectionate

_____ adventurous

_____ good at sports

_____ literary

_____ sedentary

_____ successful

_____ financially secure

_____ appreciates the finer things in life

_____ gifted and talented

_____ creative

_____ eclectic

_____ straightforward

_____ good communicator

_____ eye for art

_____ ear for music

_____ caring

_____ nurturing

_____ confident

(anything else that is important to you)

Now list your own top ten best qualities that could enhance your potential long-term partner's life.

1. _____
2. _____
3. _____
4. _____
5. _____
6. _____
7. _____
8. _____
9. _____
10. _____

Think about the mutually beneficial potential of the partnership you are already in or will eventually find. This benefit comes not from need but from appreciation of each other. What might that look like? How would it feel? Begin to define this. How might the two of you relate to each other? As kind and loving partners? Would your life be fun and yet relaxing? What kind of things would you do together? Play trivia games, mountain bike together, surf, use divination cards? Seeing and feeling your intentions are the precursors of living them in the world of magnetic attraction.

UNCOVERING YOUR DATING DESIRES

Over time, through dating, you get to know someone. When done right, the dating process illuminates your date's likes and dislikes, strengths and weaknesses. The key, of course, is "done right." That's what spiritual dating is about—doing it right. So, now that you have an idea of what kind of man you want to attract, you need to think about how you want to date him—what the process will be like for you.

First dates are great ways to see how someone acts when putting his best foot forward. A man shows you his best on a first date (you probably do the same, too!). Enjoy that fun parade of your and his best qualities.

Good first dates are lunches, dinners, coffee dates. Those activities give you time to talk and start the process of building a friendship while noticing any attraction between you and your date.

Subsequent dates can show you how you might work as a couple. Varied dating situations are like tryouts for varied life situations as a couple. You don't need to be serious about it. Just enjoy yourself and have fun while gently noticing the dynamics between you and the men you date.

Take it slowly and let a bond and friendship build between you. That is how you really get to know someone. It is important to be authentically who you are, to show yourself to your date as the bond between you builds. Hopefully, he will do the same. That way you can fall in love with each other's true self, not a best-foot-forward fabricated version.

Give yourself permission to use your instincts. If you feel in your gut that a guy is not the one for you, don't keep dating him. Move on to make room for the right guy to come into your life. Establish your feelings about exclusivity relatively early in the dating process. If you want to casually date more than one guy, be honest about it. In spiritual dating, 99 percent of the time, an agreement to be monogamous is suggested prior to any serious sexual activity.

WHAT ARE YOUR DATING DESIRES? QUIZ

1. On a first date would you rather:

    A. Have a romantic, quiet dinner
    B. Go for a hike

C. Have your tea leaves read

D. Have a beer and watch your favorite team in a local sports bar

E. Go to the trendiest wine and martini bar in town, dressed to kill

F. Go dancing at a packed club

2. You're dating someone new, and you like him. When would you be *truly* ready to sleep together?

A. Second date

B. Fourth date

C. Several weeks into regular dating

D. Two months into exclusive dating

E. Six months into the relationship

F. On your wedding night

3. You and your BF are planning your weekend. How much time would you like to spend together?

A. The whole time

B. Friday, Saturday day and night. Sunday brunch is with the girls, though

C. Just one date on Saturday with sleepover

D. Every late night after you both go out with separate friends

E. Hang out Saturday afternoon—otherwise you have plans already

F. About half the time but you need your alone time to meditate and replenish yourself

4. What word would you like to describe your next date?

A. Wild

B. Relaxing

C. Enlightening

D. Joyful

E. Stimulating

F. Fortifying

WHAT YOUR ANSWERS MEAN

Question 1: On a first date, you get to see some of things that are most important to you about your date. Your choices reflect your dating desires.

A. *Have a romantic, quiet dinner.* You can talk and connect with your guy here. You can start to see about your compatibility and if you click. You like to start sussing out the potential interpersonal connection between the two of you right away.

B. *Go for a hike.* You like to move energy—and your body. If he does too, there is potential for the two of you. You can break a sweat and see how physically fit he is and if he loves nature. Light conversation helps you start connecting without the pressure of a sit-down-and-talk scenario.

C. *Have your tea leaves read.* Right away you can see if he is open to novelty and get some potential psychic info on him. You can then segue into discussing your spirituality and even phenomena that are unexplainable, such as how right-on your readings were. In this way, the focus is on getting to know each other with an activity involved. Fun and uniqueness work for you. How about him?

D. *Have a beer and watch your favorite team in a local sports bar.* You are many guys' dream date! You are comfortable in the masculine world and like the casual feel of a low-pressure date. Your guy, if sporty, will enjoy this easy connection over shared hobbies. By staying relaxed and low-key, you can notice your date as he lets his guard down and he can do the same with you.

E. *Go to the trendiest wine and martini bar in town, dressed to kill.* You want to see how this man can hold up in his nicest suit amid scene-makers. You, and a man who enjoys this date, value status and appearances. You are both most likely successful and accomplished. You need someone who can keep up with your social and career life. Is he at home among your peers?

F. *Go dancing at a packed club.* You want to get sweaty and stimulated with your date. Dancing with him can show you a bit about his potential in bed. Physical attraction and instinct are very important to you. Do you fit together well when you dance? You need a kinesthetic and sense-filled experience to see how you feel about him. Does he smell good to you after a night of dancing? How did he feel with his arms around you in motion? What do his eyes say? You are more of a non-verbal communicator, at least initially.

Question 2: Your answer to this question is very important. It helps you define this most important step in a relationship. Your date, who becomes your BF, must be on board with this!

You're dating someone new, and you like him. When would you be truly ready to sleep together?

A. *Second date.* This means you are sexually adventurous early on in the dating process. Make sure this is authentic and emotionally healthy for you. Can you still honor your sacredness? Do you attract high-quality, respectful men? Consider how to choose the best, healthiest life for you.

B. *Fourth date.* You may be very action oriented and ready for a serious relationship. Consider taking it slow at first. What motivates you here? Hormones? Pheromones? Wanting to be liked? Or good old-fashioned desire? Does this feel right and emotionally healthy to you? Are you viewing yourself and your date as sacred? Make sure this is what is truly best for you.

C. *Several weeks into regular dating.* Gauge your emotional bond. You may intuitively feel it is right to be intimate. How close do you feel? Can you tell him almost anything? How is your friendship within your dating relationship faring?

D. *Two months into exclusive dating.* You savor the emotional bond between you before getting intimate. Is this person becoming your best friend?

E. *Six months into the relationship.* You know it is worth it to wait on getting physical in favor of emotional safety. How close to each other do you feel? Is your sexual relationship an expression of that closeness?

F. *On your wedding night.* You choose the sacred bond of marriage as your point to get intimate. You honor and respect yourself and stand strong in your beliefs. Love and commitment are your guides to intimacy.

Question 3: Your answers here give us insight into your relationship and dating style. It shows your preferred balance of together and alone time. You and your BF are planning your weekend. How much time would you like to spend together?

A. *The whole time.* When you find the right person, or someone you think is the right person, you mean it. You want to immerse yourself in your romantic relationship. It is ideal if your partner feels similarly.

B. *Friday, Saturday day and night. Sunday brunch is with the girls, though.* You have a bond with your special friends and that is important too. But mostly, you like to hang with your guy. You like the comfort level to be high with long-term dating partners.

C. *Just one date on Saturday with sleepover.* You like your own time for relaxing, recharging and socializing. Your guy is important too, but he is not the center of your life.

D. *Every late night after you both go out with separate friends.* You like a booty call! It is a relationship that allows you to hang with your friends and still have the companionship and intimacy you crave at night.

E. *Hang out Saturday afternoon—otherwise you have plans already.* Your guy is not a focus in your life. He is peripheral and that works for you. You have other interests and desires besides dating and you like to explore them.

F. *About half the time but you need your alone time to meditate and replenish yourself.* You are someone who needs recharge time. You know it is best for you to carve that out and enjoy your guy once you are rested and replenished.

Question 4: The word that you would choose to describe your next date tells us a lot about your current state of mind and heart in relationship to your life. It shows us one of the main roles you want your dates to play in your life.

A. *Wild.* You need to shake it up! And you want your dates to be a part of that excitement. You don't want to be in control too much. It is time to let loose. How can you do that safely in a healthy way for you?

B. *Relaxing.* You feel your life is busy and you like ease. Your dates ideally are times when you feel comfortable and nurtured. You seek rejuvenation. Don't discard dates that take you a bit out of your comfort zone occasionally. Make sure to keep things interesting.

C. *Enlightening.* You seek spiritual and emotional growth. Dates that integrate that kind of expansion in yourself and greater world knowledge will be enhancing for you. Take your guy to the latest talk on a topic you like or a book signing by an author you read often.

D. *Joyful.* You really prize being happy! Your dates need to echo that sentiment. Do fun stuff such as roller skating to the latest music or taking a hip-hop dance class together. Your guy needs to like to feel good, just like you!

E. *Stimulating.* Your mind, heart, and body seek new input and experiences. Dates that involve things you have never, ever done before will intrigue you. Go to an authentic Japanese tea ceremony or learn to rock climb together. A guy who introduces you to new things and provides you with engaging and thought-provoking conversation will work for you.

F. *Fortifying.* You feel the need to build yourself up. This could mean physically, emotionally, or spiritually. On a date, go to an organic cooking class and provide yourself with some quality nutrients. Be mindful of your emotional strength and go to a feel-good movie that will give you heart. Or spiritually fortify yourselves by going to a service at the local Buddhist temple. Seek the nourishment you need and make sure you don't exclusively depend on guys to provide that. Find it within!

If more than one answer appeals to you on certain questions, it just means that you have a few sides to yourself in regard to that topic. You can choose multiple answers for one question. There are no rules!

DEFINE YOUR LOVE LIFE

Your love life is defined as the way you dance with love in all of its forms. This includes dates and all kinds of relationships: romantic, familial, and friendships. You exchange some level of love with most people you connect closely with. With romances, of course, love is brewing (or not) from the get-go. How that love brew steeps is up to you and your partner. In a way, it is a matter of taste.

Is your desire for your love life that it be a full partnership between equals? A spiritual dance of light and life? Or a satisfying, but not time consuming, part of the whole? Again the question "What do you want?" is being asked with a twist.

What do you want your love life to feel like? Be like? What do you want it to ignite in you or comfort in you?

As you figure out what you are looking for in relationships, you can set about lightly living—simply allowing your needs and wants to be met in the perfect timing. This part requires some faith, in yourself and in life.

Creating space for love in your life just feels good and it effortlessly draws love to you. You can't really stop it. Remember, we talked about Natural Law of dating in Chapter 1? Giving love out sends more back to you. That Law applies to life, too. Meaningful personal relationships are the bread and butter of a full love life. An iPad doesn't replace a hug or a friend to talk to. In what way could you cultivate love in your life?

Later in the chapter, you are going to make a Roadmap to follow to keep your love life on track. Let's start by exploring some ideas you may have about romantic relationships.

WHERE DO YOU WANT TO GO?

These questions will help you figure out where you're going on your dating journey.

Do you feel that it is for your highest good for you to have sex with dates you do not feel deep love for? No judgments are being made here. If you do, that's fine.

Are you ultimately envisioning yourself married or its equivalent? If so, what does that partnership look and feel like?

- Is it spiritual?
- Emotionally healthy and rich?
- Passionate and satisfying?
- Comforting?
- Fun and keeps you on your toes?
- What else?

Do you want to have children with your soul mate one day?

Do you see yourself in a serious relationship long-term but not married?

Do you want to be more of a free agent who feels romantically fulfilled?

Are you unsure about your sexual orientation?

Do you feel like you need more time for experimentation before getting into something long-term?

Ask yourself these questions to get a clearer picture of your perfect love life. That is what we want you to be living. Remember the important role self-love plays in this whole equation. It is paramount.

You are now defining your sales order in detail. This breeds more self-awareness, too. All of this consciousness is melding together to recreate your love life. In time, you will see the fruit blooming forth on your growing tree of awareness. Tend it. Nurture your being through this time of reinventing yourself.

WHAT ABOUT YOUR NEEDS?

If you can fill your needs without having a guy in your life, that is the best way to be. Your life and satisfaction won't be dependent on anyone but you. How freeing! Then when the right guy shows up, and you and he are ready, you can spot him and be an alluring, confident, fulfilled women to be desired, loved, and valued.

Your needs—sexual, emotional, mental, social, and sensual—are real. The key to your happiness is to validate all of your needs. If you do this yourself, you are left wanting for nothing. You are independent and full. There will still be space in your life for your soul mate, but he won't show up and find you a needy mess. Acknowledge your needs. Then determine how to fill them while honoring your sacred beauty.

SEXUAL

Do not underestimate the power of a vibrator. Suddenly, your satisfaction is in your hands. You can explore your sexuality this way and be as spiritual, or not, as you wish. Filling this need yourself is especially healthy. Not only does it make you release all kinds of endorphins and happiness-boosting chemicals, but you don't require a man for sexual satisfaction. No longer will sexual frustration motivate you to be intimate with someone you'd be better off keeping some distance from. No longer will you have sex when it is not the right time or the right person. Instead, you can make conscious sexual choices that are best for you.

EMOTIONAL

Tap into your network of heart friends and family. If those existing people are not the kind you want to share your feelings with, cultivate new friendships with like-minded people. If you have some issues to talk about, consider a therapist of some kind. Determine how to fill your emotional needs. Sometimes pets can help with that. You can share unconditional love with animals. Visit friends' pets or volunteer to walk dogs at a local shelter—whatever resonates for you. Just get in touch with any unfulfilled emotional needs so you won't fall into a relationship simply because you are craving companionship.

MENTAL

Try book clubs, conversation, and trivia game night with friends. Toastmasters' public-speaking groups are a fun way to meet people in an intellectual setting. Meetup.com has groups for all types of cerebral pursuits. Exercise your mind. Chitchat in coffee houses or with coworkers. Go to lectures at your local college or university. Take classes, whether on cooking, ceramics, bookbinding, calculus, or writing science fiction. These situations will stimulate your mind.

SOCIAL

Being social is not just cruising Facebook. It is having meaningful and fun interactions with people. Roller skate with friends. Take your nieces and nephews bowling. Go to wine tastings. Whatever you enjoy, share it with others. Reach out to people. Fill your social needs.

SENSUAL

Your sensual needs can be filled by you. Take a warm, fragrant bubble bath. Smell luscious flowers you send yourself. Paint and create with abandon. Tap into your creative energy and make it manifest. Make love to yourself after giving yourself an essential oil foot massage. Redecorate your home with a passionate and sensual theme.

When you take ownership of fulfilling your needs, you put the power in your own hands. You do not need a date or partner to be happy and satisfied. He is just the icing on the cake.

CREATE YOUR LOVE LIFE ROADMAP

It's time to create your Love Life Roadmap. This will give you a quick reference guide to help you make conscious dating choices. Instead of continuing on your dating path without any kind of directions to follow, you will have a map with lots of possible routes on hand. You won't be trying to follow an amorphous and vague idea of what you want.

Start with a large piece of paper or poster board. It can be white or any other color you can write on with markers or colored pencils. You can be as artistic and crafty with this roadmap as you would like. You can add pictures from magazines that speak to you. You can draw things. You can use color to represent textures and ideas. You can glue on objects that are meaningful to you: photocopies of pictures or your passport to symbolize international travel, charms or feathers, string, yarn, luxe fabrics, anything that speaks to you and evokes something you want to manifest in your love life. If you don't consider yourself artistic or crafty, you can just do a plain, but still very powerful, version of your Love Life Roadmap.

Your Love Life Roadmap should reflect you—who you are and your essence should be apparent in this creation. So should your dating style and your dating desires. By looking at it we should also be able to easily see where you would like your love life to be in a year, five years, and so forth.

So, gather your art materials. Get ready to make some magic!

State out loud, "I will now make my Love Life Roadmap for my highest good. I ask that it be infused with power and magnetism and that the process and outcomes be joyful."

Lay out your paper or poster board horizontally (long way across). Keep in mind that these instructions are just a suggestion. If you feel the urge to do something else in your creative process, go for it! Trust the power of this creative exercise. Everything you put in this "power image" is enlivened by the power of alchemy. You are a wizard today! You are manifesting magic.

Use a pencil (you might erase these lines later) to divide the paper into six even square areas, three on top and three on the bottom. Write the titles below, one to each area, using whatever color and script feels most representative of its mood.

1. The top left area is titled *What I Want*.
2. The top middle area is titled *I Love Me*.
3. The top right area is titled *My First Dates*.
4. The bottom left area is titled *My Dating Desires*.
5. The bottom middle area is titled *My Radiant Love Life*.
6. The bottom right area is titled *Where I Want My Love Life to End Up*.

If you have gathered some pictures from the Internet or magazines that speak to you, place them on the paper where they fit in light of your titled areas.

1. Now let's work on each area. Start with the *What I Want* square. Go back to the section of this chapter titled "Know What You Want." In that section, I asked you some questions: What do you want? What *else* do you want? What do you crave emotionally? Put your answers to those questions in this square.

   Next, write down your top ten qualities out of the forty-five listed under "Your Ideal Partner's Most Important Qualities." You can put these all in the box in creative ways with lots of colors and pictures. Make it your own. Include anything else that comes to mind or heart for you. This square is about what you want. Decorate it and infuse it with creative power. You are going to draw to you what is in this square.

2. Now let's create the *I Love Me* square. This area is front and center and it is all about the many reasons you love yourself. In this box somewhere include a beautiful picture of yourself. Just you. You are the focus of this section. Cut out words from magazines that describe you and your wonderfulness. Combine them in new ways. Words like *luminous, beauty, goddess, healthy, laughing, angel, happy, magical, adventure, halo, calm, welcome, flower, romance, treasure, believe, inspiration, euphoria.* Words and pictures that evoke you. Write words in, too, and add drawings and symbols as you would like. Devote this area to how great you are. And make sure you title it prominently, *I Love Me.* You can also write in some affirmations. Here are some great examples:

- "I love myself unconditionally."
- "I accept myself totally and see my beauty radiating through my life."
- "I am spiritual perfection, just as I am."
- "I am my highest self."
- "I appreciate myself."
- "I am wonderful."
- "I am a magical person who is blessed in each moment."

Decorate this square and celebrate yourself. You have to celebrate yourself so that others can celebrate you, too. Self-love is powerful. You are giving yourself a major life-enhancing gift.

3. Next, the *My First Dates* section. What do you look for in an enjoyable first date? Go back to the "Dating Desires" quiz earlier in this chapter. The first question asked you what you would like to do on a first date. Look back at the explanation for your answer. It tells you about your first-date desires and personal-

ity. Use that info and give some more thought to your best first dates. What do you want your next first date(s) to be like? Illustrate that in this square. Use colors and cut out pictures that look like good first-date-type spots and happy couples on first dates. Convey the feelings you want to feel on your next first date—and how you want him to feel, too. Include anything that feels right for this section and decorate it in anticipation and excitement for your next first date. It might be your last first date, in the best possible way, and with the power from creating this square it will be good!

4. Now, the *My Dating Desires* square. Go back to the "Dating Desires" quiz earlier in the chapter. You were asked three more questions:

   1. You're dating someone new, and you like him. When would you be truly ready to sleep together?
   2. You and your BF are planning your weekend. How much time would you like to spend together?
   3. What word would you like to describe your next date?

Look back at each answer and the explanation that was given. Record that information in this section. You are creating a graphic and linguistic representation of how you would like your dating life to be. Keep it positive. Instead of writing "No boring dates that waste my time," write "Fun and interesting dates that are productive for my love life."

Fill this area with all that an ideal dating life would be for you. Put down what you wish for in your dates. Include how often you want to see your dates. Do you like more alone time? Or do you love having a loving partner with you most of the time? Make the section beautiful; it embodies your future dating life. Embellish it. Create it with love.

5. *My Radiant Love Life* comes next. This square will show all of the beauty you want in your love life. Go back to the section in this chapter titled "Define Your Love Life." Look through the questions. Include your answers in this area of your Love Life Roadmap.

   Paint that picture in this part of your roadmap. Use color, texture, pictures, words. Fill it up with joy and good fortune! Create!

6. Lastly, create the section of the roadmap called *Where I Want My Love Life to End Up*. This square will show whether you want to be married one day. You can include when, too. Know that divine timing may be a bit different; have faith that it is the best and for your highest good. Make sure you create it to be joyful and beautiful, just like you'd like your life to be. This is the destination you are manifesting; your future soon becomes your present. Think big! Create!

7. Now that your Love Life Roadmap is ready, take a look at it. Does it need more of a certain color? More joy energy? Make the necessary artistic and mood-feeling adjustments.

When you feel it is complete, hover your hands over it and say aloud, "I now activate My Love Life Roadmap. It is empowered and infused with deep magic and complete, loving power. I allow myself to be propelled to my destination. It is done and I am grateful."

You are done! Good job, you conscious dater, you!

Part Three

Manifest Your Man

In the previous parts, we've talked about how to get ready to consciously date by looking at your past dating experiences and by understanding how your background—including your family life—may have caused you to make choices that weren't so great for you. We talked about how to clear those effects from your dating life so that you can go forward, open to new possibilities and not repeating the same patterns.

We've also discussed how to put into practice the principles of spiritual dating. Once you've committed to a new way of dating, to being respectful of yourself and others, authentic in your actions, and willing to grow, you're ready to take the next step—manifesting your man.

In this part, we'll discuss how to bring your soul mate—or at least a man worth dating—into your life by identifying what you're looking for. In Chapter 5, you'll learn how to appreciate the sacredness in yourself—and in your ideal man. You'll form an idea of what you want right now—and what you imagine you'll want in the future. We'll talk about the dos and don'ts of spiritual dating and look at some case histories of how some women manifested their soul mates.

In Chapter 6, you'll learn that you can date in your own way and on your own terms by becoming a dating nonconformist. You'll find out what that can look like. We'll also discuss how to set boundaries in spiritual dating, and how to indulge in the fun parts of the dance, such as flirting, without misleading anyone. Finally, we'll dig into ways to use your intuition to know when someone is worth dating.

Are you ready to meet your soul mate? Let's get started!

Chapter Five
Sacred Dating

You are sacred. Your body is sacred. Your heart is sacred. Your mind is sacred. Your spirit is sacred. What does sacred mean? It means blessed, revered, protected, connected with the divine. It means that you are made of the divine. Of stardust, of purity, and of passion. In your relationship with yourself, this shows up in your unconditional acceptance and love for your true, authentic self. You see yourself as sacred and therefore accept yourself and your innate divine beauty. Because of your sacredness you treat yourself with love and kindness and fill your needs, just as we talked about in Chapter 4.

That is premise one of spiritual dating: You are sacred.

Premise two is: your dates are sacred, also. Their bodies, minds, hearts, and souls are so very sacred. Do they recognize their own sacredness? To be conscious daters, they need to.

If your date recognizes his sacredness and has plenty of self-respect, there is good potential that he can see your sacredness, too. Seeing other people's sacredness is a natural follow-up to seeing your own. Then, and only then, can the two of you consciously date. That is the essence of spiritual dating. As we discussed in Chapter 3, conscious dating happens when you are your authentic self with the goal of making a real, honest connection with your dates.

How can you tell if someone recognizes his sacredness and yours? It often takes spending some time together. As you get to know someone, notice how he talks about himself. Does he speak about himself respectfully? Does he engage in a lot of negative self-talk? (Stuff like "I am such a tool sometimes, I never remember to file my reports on time at work. I'm stupid.") Does he engage in degrading talk about other people? (Like "My ex was such a bitch, she would nag me day and night. Once she turned into an old bitch, I ditched her." Or a more subtle version, like "Dean is so fat and gross he can't get dates.") Unkindness behind someone's back can be a sign of a lack of respect for other people in general—and that could affect you.

Conscious people usually have an outlook that is positive overall. Stressful instances sometimes provoke negative responses; we are still human, after all. But an overarching respect and regard for life, family and friends, plants and animals is a good indicator of a conscious person.

That kind of respect for you plays out in the way he is present, listening 100 percent to what you are saying. Valuing your opinion. Behaving in a considerate manner toward you. Respecting your time, attention, and energy. You can feel he values and respects you and see his kind, respectful behavior toward everyone from waitstaff that serve you dinner to people in line for a movie with you. Respect is a precursor for seeing sacredness.

So, if you are on a date with a respectful man who behaves with kindness and compassion, then you can look for his sacredness-vision, his ability to see sacredness. Remember, in this book sacredness is spiritual but not religious; you're not necessarily looking for someone who has a specific religious point of view, but rather one who is open to the spiritual and can see it in himself and in you. Once you begin to get to know your date, you can approach the topic. Explain your take on the sacredness topic in a way that resonates for you and ask him his feelings and thoughts on the topic.

SACREDNESS-VISION AND SPIRITUAL COMPATIBILITY

Because you are a spiritual woman, seeking to be a spiritual dater with a spiritual man, it's important to define the who, what, and how of this equation.

WHO

1. You

- What does spirituality and sacredness mean to you personally?
- What are your spiritual views?
- Do you believe in past, future, infinite lives?
- Heaven and hell?
- Just kindness and love?
- Do you have a life's purpose you feel you are here to fulfill?
- Do you believe most people have a life's purpose or purposes? How important is that belief to you?
- Is spiritually giving back to the world important to you?
- Do you believe you give back to the world just by being conscious and kind?
- Do you follow your intuition?
- Do you see the sacredness in all life? Do you want to continue developing your sacredness-vision?
- Define your views and core spiritual values.

2. Him

If you are currently living a spiritual life and seeking to live an ever-evolving spiritual life long-term, then your mate must be at minimum tolerant of that and ideally in harmony with it.

- Worldview-wise, what does your ideal mate believe spiritually?
- How intuitive is he?

- Does he express his spirituality?
- How?
- Is his spirituality and intuition a major part of his life?
- What are ideal ways this would be displayed by him?
- Does your ideal mate have a strong sense of life's purpose?
- Does he have a drive to give back?
- Does he set intentions and magnetize them?
- Is he rooted in love and kindness?
- Does he see the sacredness of all life? Is his sacredness-vision strong?
- What else is he like spiritually?

Someone recently answered this question in a simpler way as "He needs to be as insane as I am and have a purpose." She values life purpose and "insane" probably speaks to her spiritual worldview. She wants a guy who sees the spiritual world similarly to the way she does and is driven to be of service.

WHAT

- What will your spiritual selves interacting look like?
- How similar would you like your views to be?
- How will this affect your life together?

As an example, I can say to my husband, "My intuition tells me . . ." and he gets it. He honors it and has been known to say the same thing back. We both value our intuition and believe in it. We sometimes make life and marital decisions based upon it and are both completely happy with that. If I were with someone who didn't understand that, it would be a major part of myself I could never really share and have him get. That is spiritual compatibility.

What would you like spiritual compatibility to be like for you and your soul mate? What is ideal spiritual compatibility for you?

HOW

- How can you tell if you are spiritually compatible with someone and if they have great sacredness-vision?

1. Conversation

You can talk about your views of the world and spirituality and notice how they complement each other. Discussion in the beginning phases shows so much!

You can talk about your personal views, what sacredness and spirituality mean to you, and see what he feels about those topics, too.

2. Observation

You can observe whether he treats life as sacred. If he sees a frog hopping on the road in a rainstorm and aims his car to run it over, that would be a no on the sacredness-vision.

After a date, look at this exercise.

1. Did you clearly represent your spiritual self as defined above?

   - Does he match any of the spiritual qualities listed above as desirable for him to have?
   - Can you see the what of your two lives meshing?

2. Can you see the how of his spirituality and do you resonate with it? Does it feel good to you? Could you discuss this with him next time?

LET'S GET PHYSICAL—OR NOT

It is a good idea to keep from getting physically serious until you have sussed out if your date sees your body—and his—as sacred. Spiritual dating is frequently taken slowly physically, at least at first. This is because of your deep respect for yourselves and each other. Two conscious daters know that sexual activity is an expression of love between two people. It can be raunchy and wild, or tender and sweet, but it still springs forth from love. Can your guy hang with that and is it how he feels things should be? If yes, then you are onto something good.

Spiritual daters may not have always been that way. Our pasts are as varied as our likes and dislikes. Sometimes years of disrespectful dating and sexual experiences inspire us to try a new way of being. The sacred way. Sacred daters are not born-again virgins. We accept and embrace our pasts as part of the path that shaped who we are now. We might even look back fondly on some of our passionate highlights. But now, we have gotten to the point where we want those ecstatic passions served up with a heaping dose of respectful love and regard. And they are even better when they are sacred. Sacred orgasms are more powerful and satisfying, sacred lovemaking is more rich and pleasurable, sacred dating is more fun and aligned with our emotional maturity. We just have to sometimes be a bit more patient for timing to bring us a sacred dating partner. We will talk a lot more about sacred lovemaking in Chapter 10.

HOW DO I CONSCIOUSLY DATE?

As a woman who recognizes your sacredness and owns your sexuality with love and joy, how will you go on dates? Or *find* dates, for that matter? Where are the conscious men? They're everywhere.

They are a portion of the men you see every day. Sometimes it might seem like they're a small portion of typical guys. It depends on the quality of your interactions lately.

A Mother's Wisdom

When I was twenty-nine, I was driving to the bachelorette party of yet another friend getting married. I talked with my mom on the phone (using a headset for safety!) on the way. I was frustrated. Lamenting that I wasn't married yet, I questioned whether men who were spiritual and conscious, the type of man I wanted to date, were out there. I questioned whether they even existed. My mom said, "There only needs to be one."

It is true. Ultimately, there only needs to be one great, stellar, cosmic match for you. It took three more years of reasonably uneventful dating until I met my husband. And as the cliché goes, the stars aligned and we knew without reservation we wanted to be together.

I had to be ready for my husband, and on the way to that bachelorette party I still wasn't quite ready. I had put together a lovely recipe. I had begun to mix the ingredients of self-love and self-awareness, but cosmic timing had its own agenda. He had to be ready, too. At the time of the aforementioned bachelorette party, he was very busy with a demanding career and would have been challenged to be deeply present to the magic that was to occur between us.

Whatever you are looking for in a date or relationship, trust the timing to be perfect. Prepare yourself by cleaning your emotional house and enjoying your life. You will find exactly what you need at the exact right time. It is a fact. Trust it.

In the meantime, allow heart-centered conscious men to befriend you. Trust your instincts and be clear about how sacred you are. See what happens. Continue to learn and grow, working through old patterns that might clutter your energetic field.

If you are asked on a date and you feel like saying yes, do it. You can date for fun, to meet new people, and enjoy yourself, whether or not your companion is conscious-date material. However, remember that even swapping spit with someone scrambles a bit of their energy into yours. That means conscious kissing is a good idea, too!

Have fun and also have the highest standards for your heart. That is really what we are talking about here. The heart. Your heart is sacred, beautiful. It may be bruised, in recovery. It may be any degree of open or closed. Meet it. Love it. Be present to your heart.

To consciously date, simply use your clear heart. Place your hands over your heart and go into it, feeling present. Ask your heart what it wants. Ask if a particular date is for your highest good. Ask your loving heart anything. The secret to conscious dating is letting your heart be your guide.

SPIRITUAL DATING DOS AND DON'TS

A list of guidelines outlining what is and is not sacred dating is helpful when you are in the midst of new dating experiences. You can consult this list before a new date to prepare yourself to break old dating patterns that no longer work for you. You can look this over after a date to see if the date was on track with your sacred dating mindset. Take from the list what works for you.

SPIRITUAL DATING	
Dating Dos	**Dating Don'ts**
Trust your instincts.	Go against your gut feelings.
Present your authentic self.	Mold yourself toward your date's apparent preferences.
Be confident in who you are.	Be intimidated by new surroundings and people.
Affirm your sacredness through your actions.	Get caught up in hormones at the expense of good decisions.
Be present in your heart space during dates.	Waste your energy if there is not a heart resonance; move on (consider being platonic friends).
Look for the sacred in your dates.	Always judge a book by its cover; use your heart to see your dates.
Have major fun.	Be too serious about the whole dating thing.
Honor yourself and your needs.	Push through four more hours in stilettos if your body is telling you it is time to call it a night.
Consider dating against your type.	Date the same type of guy over and over.
Try new things. Give your date's interests a chance.	Do *everything* your date wants to.
Notice his spiritual views as you get to know each other.	Expect to be *exactly* the same on everything.
Ask him what is important to him, what he wants out of life.	Assume he thinks the way you do.
Notice whether you feel a thrill when you touch.	Go nuts with that spark if the sacredness is not established.
Be present to his kiss.	Continue making out if it doesn't feel absolutely 100 percent right.
Enjoy passionate connections to the fullest.	Go overboard too soon.
Listen to what he says and how he says it.	Miss out on seeing his true essence.

SPIRITUAL DATING	
Notice whether he listens to you with all of his attention.	Hide your true essence.
Look into his eyes and see his soul.	Challenge him to a staring contest without telling him first.
Be open to love.	Jump into lust and mistake it for love.
Meet his friends in time. They tell a lot about him.	Discount the facts. If his crowd is full of piggish, porn-watching types, he is at least comfortable around that energy.
After a while, imagine the two of you together long-term.	Mentally plan your wedding after two dates.
Notice how he treats his mother.	Pin everything on that if she is crazy or has major issues.

DATING DISASTERS

Sometimes a date is not what we hoped. At times, dates can even be disastrous. When they are hilariously disastrous, they make a great story. When they are detrimental to our well-being, we must learn from them so as not to repeat them.

MENTAL CASE

Frank asked out Nanette after chatting her up at a wine bar. Her friends were a bit wary of him, thinking he was too slick. She thought he was so handsome and interesting—even intellectual. Nanette liked smart, successful men. Frank was all that and more.

They went on their first date at a book signing. Their second was at a Holocaust museum. For the third date, they went for dinner and back to Frank's architectural marvel of a house. They looked out over hills and valleys through walls of windows and talked more literature.

Nanette started to turn the conversation toward their families, lives, more personal things. Frank turned it back to academic topics. What started as a natural volley became a verbal tug of war. Nanette wanted to know him. She wanted to go deeper. He kept talking about work, current events, or the latest cultural trends. This went on for hours! It was exhausting. Nanette left after turning down the pass he made at her.

She got home tired and annoyed. She went to her list of qualities she wanted in a man and amended "high IQ and intellectually focused" to "mentally my equal and a diverse conversationalist."

Maybe Frank was emotionally stunted. Maybe he was afraid of being vulnerable. Maybe he just liked to talk surface and intellectual and then have sex. She would never know but she did know to move on after a frustrating night. She could tell the compatibility wasn't there.

Lesson: It often takes a few dates to determine basic compatibility—whether you could be friends with someone and enjoy your time together.

THE ANTI-FAIRYTALE

James and Suzie lived near each other, and with perfect weather forecast, agreed to walk to a quiet neighborhood restaurant together. As they walked down the street, her heel broke. She stumbled and cursed like a sailor. After picking up replacement shoes at her house, they tried again.

Then it started raining—hard. A cab was approaching and James manfully stepped out to hail it. It drove by without stopping and hit a puddle, soaking him from head to toe. They ran the rest of the way to dinner. As they got in sight of their destination, Suzie's foot hit a slick of motor oil and she slid offbalance, heading for the pavement.

James caught her arm and hauled her to her feet. It started to pour torrentially. They ran to the door, dripping and soaked.

After they dried off, they were able to have a pleasant meal. They found they had a lot in common and enjoyed each other's company. At the end of the meal, James insisted on paying only to find out minutes later that his card was declined. Suzie quickly took care of the bill, with James protesting and embarrassed.

In spite of all that, she admired his spunk. He was quirky. And she had kind of had fun. So when he invited her back to his apartment, she went. They got in the door and she was immediately covered in dog hair and slobber by his three large terriers. They jumped on her barking and one vigorously humped her leg. James corralled the dogs and settled Suzie onto the couch with some wine. They talked more and he leaned in for a kiss.

The phone rang and he looked into her eyes, "The machine will get it."

"Hi James, it's your mother. Why aren't you answering? Where are you? I talked to Aunt Sophia and she asked Uncle Milt and he said your rash needs to be checked out. Has it cleared up yet? Call me back, James," a nasal voice whined from the answering machine speaker.

"Oh my gosh," James put his head in his hands. "This date has been a disaster."

Suzie didn't know what to say. It had. After a minute she said, "Well, it hasn't been dull. I had fun with you."

"Good. So, that was my caricature of a mother," James laughed. "And for the record, the rash was on my hand because I spilled battery acid on it while trying to rewire a car battery. And as you can see, it's gone."

He laid his hand on her knee, "No more rash." Their eyes caught and he leaned in again. This time he kissed her gently, just a light brush of the lips. She shivered. He wrapped his arms around her. "Let's warm you up."

Engulfed in James's arms Suzie felt good. Right. He kissed her again, deeper. One of the dogs jumped up on the couch and panted in their ears watching them kiss. They giggled.

"He wants to be included," smiled James. "Go to the den, Bailey." The dog trotted away.

"I think we should try this again tomorrow night. Rain or shine. Shoes or no. You and me are the only necessary ingredients. What d'you think?"

And they did. Next time and many more, James paid, held cab doors and behaved like a chivalrous wonder. Two years later they were married at a happy ceremony with the nasal mother, the three terriers, and all of their family and friends.

Lesson: Sometimes a bad date is not a disaster. It can be a blessing.

SPIRITUAL DATING SUCCESS

There is nothing like a nice heart-warming story of love to keep you going and open your heart. Reading how other people have experienced love, romance, and passion, all in ways that affirm their sacredness, gives us a blueprint for the emotions of falling in spiritual love. The people in the story below were self-aware. They had consistently made a commitment to their own personal growth and emotional maturity. They were ready to find a true love partner and also a spiritual mate. Enjoy!

FIRE AND WATER

Rainbow Blaze was a new age buff. She was a gifted clairvoyant and a shaman. As a passionate spirit, she was prone to high emotions. At her center for yoga and the healing arts, she met Dave.

Dave was a well-respected workshop presenter. His life's mission was feeding the hungry and creating peaceable classrooms for children. Dave was a gentle spirit, a water sprite of sorts. He enlivened each space he entered with love and his melodic singing and speaking voice. Animals and children loved him.

He arrived to teach a workshop at the center and her heart felt like it literally skipped a beat when she saw him. They shook hands. The jolt of electricity when they touched was powerful. Colorful fire met melodic water and they looked at each other, still holding hands. Rainbow found her voice. "Hi, Dave. It is really wonderful to meet you."

They chatted for a few more minutes about how much he loved the center and how it was great that the waiting list for his workshops was so long. Then he asked her to go to dinner with him Sunday night after the retreat completed. She said yes.

They sat down and had a great dinner with amazing conversation. The cozy round booth put them next to each other. Throughout the night they got a bit closer. By the time they shared a dessert, they were sitting side by side with their knees touching under the table. Both were in a state of happy shock by what they were feeling. It was a buzz that had nothing to do with the glass of wine they shared.

They left to take a walk along the river path winding through the town. Holding hands and contented, they walked mostly quiet for awhile. A bench came upon their path and they sat, looked in each other's eyes, and just had to kiss. A soft summer wind blew and a nearby tree rained tiny white flower petals on them. It felt like nature was embracing them, too.

It was a perfect date. It wasn't about fanfare, bells and whistles, or huge grand gestures. It was two people of a similar, spiritual mindset who recognized their own and each other's sacredness.

Two people who were ready, interacting with kindness and an openness to love. You will hear the rest of Rainbow and Dave's story in Part 6, so stay tuned.

SET YOUR SACRED DATING INTENTIONS

Set some affirmative intentions now based on what you learned in this chapter.

Fill in the blanks as needed and repeat aloud:

1. "I choose to consciously date and be a sacred dater."

   - "I am sacred."
   - "I demonstrate my sacredness to myself when I _____ ."
   - "I see love in everything and affirm it in my life."

2. "I receive the blessing of past dates, the lessons and the joy, and let the rest go now for all time."

Now create an affirmative statement that sums up the spiritual compatibility you want with your next partner.

1. "My next partner and I will be spiritually compatible. That will look like _____ ."

   - "I will from this point forth only date people who see me as sacred and that I see as sacred. This will be easy and joyful. I am grateful for this choice and its gifts in my life. So be it."

2. Set any more dating intentions using affirmative statements that you feel moved to set.

Chapter Six
How to Date Anew

Dating in a spiritual way may be brand-new for you. It certainly is not the norm and we do not see a lot of it mentioned in the media. Typically, we see women putting on a front as to who they are supposed to be and acting as if they don't care as much as they actually do. Or they may breeze through guys with a closed and wounded heart. Instead, you have an opportunity to be authentic and real. You can be you, no pretenses, just your hot, wild, nurturing, true self. You will find that it feels good. It feels right to date from a place of self-honoring. Let's dive in and explore how to date anew.

HOW TO BE A DATING NONCONFORMIST

The first thing you need to know is that you are not going to date like your other single girlfriends anymore. You are going to be a dating nonconformist. Get ready for that. Sometimes you may feel like you relate less to the usual dating stories—the hookups, the bad behavior tolerated by busy women, the low standards, the pickiness about all the wrong things. Nonconformity in dating is all about being authentic and true to yourself.

DECIDING WHAT WORKS—AND WHAT DOESN'T

What conformist parts of dating would you like to chuck?

- Sex on the third date? Yay or nay?
- The guy always paying? Does that feel authentic to you?
- Seeing each other with a frequency of routine? Does that work for you?
- Guys only asking girls out? Would you like to do the asking?
- Just hanging out/friends with benefits?
- Texting instead of calling? Do you like the time-saving aspect of this or not?
- Meeting out late at bars in college substituting for dates? Does that feel sacred and good to you?
- Skype sex when one of you is traveling? Oh, yeah! Or no way?
- Dancing around commitment or jumping into it? Do either of those bother you?
- Dating leading to relationship leading to marriage? Is that the trajectory that resonates for you if you were with the right person?
- Coffee dates to start? Boring? Do you even like coffee?
- Lunch dates if either of you is not sure if it's friendship or romance?

What would you rather do? This isn't a quiz with right and wrong answers.

NONCONFORMITY IN ACTION

In earlier chapters, you identified your dating desires. Now nonconformity is required to put them into action. Be strong and solid in your uniqueness. If you are looking for a rare, spiritual, interesting, emotionally mature man who is right for you, then you are going to need to be different from the average woman who is dating. You are going to need to truly be your amazing, exotic, interesting (possibly eccentric) self. You can weed out the overly conventional dudes with your unconventional attitude. Let go of the fear of not fitting in. You belong here. You are uniquely you. And that is perfection. Period. Use your newfound confidence (from Chapter 3) to help you date in nonconformist ways.

Do not do anything in your dating life that does not feel 100 percent right to you. If social convention dictates that you do something that does not work for you, buck the system. Don't do whatever it is.

Always be kind is your only mantra in this. There is usually a kind way to handle any dating situation that needs some nonconformity. Do not be motivated by the fear of not fitting in or of your date not liking you. If he is the right date for you, he will support the fullness of who you are and want you 110 percent comfortable and happy.

Nonconformist dating skips a lot of the obligation of dating and jumps into a sacred way of relating. It is honestly communicating and honoring each other's needs and wants. It is choosing joy and fun together and prizing spiritual exploration. Doesn't that sound nice?

Declare yourself a dating nonconformist now. Choose freedom and joy!

FLIRTING WITH BOUNDARIES

Dating almost always entails flirting, the playful way that you explore the possibility of romantic interchange. It is the witty banter between people who like each other, the touch on the arm to punctuate a conversation point, the lowered eyes that unconsciously convey potential romantic interest. Flirting is safe. It doesn't have to lead to anything. It is just a dipping of the toe into the pool of potential romance.

Flirting is especially fun when you have embraced your sexual persona and you feel confident. Lots of women tell me they feel empowered when they flirt with men and get the reaction they are looking for. Sometimes women out at a bar may flirt more for sport than because they are looking to make a connection.

At its best, flirting is a respectful, playful way of interacting romantically without any pressure. In the dating world, flirting in the initial stages of meeting and even during early dating is best done consciously. Choosing your flirtations consciously shows potential romantic interest. It indicates a desire to make a bit of a connection and see how that feels.

When you see yourself and others as sacred, you usually skip flirting for sport. It is always good to remember the precept of being kind. Can you flirt with kindness? When you flirt consciously, you are flirting with appropriate boundaries. That means in a way that is energetically safe for you. Boundaries in this case mean flirting in proportion to how romantically interested you are in the guy and him in you. It also means in a way that is appropriate and energetically safe. For example, being drunk in a bar and rubbing the entire front of your body on a guy you just met is energetically not safe. The guy may be psyched and all over you, too. Even so, you are energetically vulnerable when your flirting actions are disproportionate for the situation and when they are over the top with new guys you don't know yet. On the other hand, if you meet a new guy and do the usual hair tosses, sparkling conversation with a bit of eye-batting type stuff in proportion to how you are feeling about him, you are flirting with appropriate boundaries.

THE DOWNSIDE OF FLIRTING

When our boundaries are not clear, we can leak our vital life force, and less conscious folks may take it. Here is an example. Suppose you meet someone and the two of you feel a connection. He's not conscious of it, but he feels needy; his emotional state is raw. Perhaps he has had a bad week and is feeling tired and sad because he had a bad run-in with his drug-addicted dad. He thinks you are attractive. You can be kind to him with very appropriate boundaries and no detrimental energy exchange will happen. You two might chat with you both respecting each other's personal space, not touching or acting flirty. Just being friends. The very initial stages of getting to know someone. Your intuition, if working well, might make you feel not inclined to flirt with him. Usually he will take the cue from you and be appropriate too.

On the other hand, were you to flirt with him with no real intention of having a romantic relationship with him, then you would open the door for him to siphon away some of your vital life force. You get physically closer, you send him signals that say "Maybe." To most guys, "maybe" means that there is a chance. You act the way society has shown you to act toward attractive men—flirty, tinkling laughs, hair tosses, eye contact. It is a vibe. Flirting opens a door to greater energy exchange. So just from flirting, guys may unconsciously take some of your vital life force. But if you aren't actually interested in them, that should not be happening. When you are intentionally flirting, the exchange is mutual. When you are flirting and don't mean it, you are giving your energy away to someone whose energy you don't want to receive back. That is why it is a good idea to maintain appropriate boundaries. Flirt when you mean it, not when you do not or aren't sure but probably do not.

Here is another example. In a bar, all kinds of flirting happens. Alcohol is flowing, and boundaries are already relaxed. In fact, alcohol consumption does something very marked to your energy bodies that you need to know about. It opens up your second (or navel) chakra (energy center). The more you drink, the less inhibited you are, right? You are like a beacon, like one of those lights to attract moths, and this beacon is located right in your abdomen, your sexual center. (It is right in front of and woven through your uterus.) This light, when unhealthily open during alcohol consumption, is like a dense energy attractor.

Earlier in this section we talked about the way energy attracts other energy and is exchanged via flirting. Some energy has a higher vibration than others. If energy is highly vibrational, it enhances your physical and emotional health. It is good for you. There are people who are happy and calm that you just feel good around; those people probably have higher vibrational, lighter energy. Dense energy is lower vibrational. It exists and that is okay. It is not innately bad, but it isn't something that you want interacting with your own energy field. If it does, it may bring your vibration down. As a result you may feel grouchier, less happy while around it or afterward, more tired and generally less vital. In extreme cases it may adversely affect your health. It gathers in bars and places where alcohol is being consumed. It is attracted there by all of the open sources of higher vibrational energy—in this case, all of the open bellies full of vital life force.

This same concept applies in bars. Consider the situation with the same guy who was feeling needy and found you attractive in the example a couple of paragraphs ago. Put both of you in a bar situation where you were drinking and feeling loose. Maybe you shot him a brief look. Your flirting, and your open chakras and energy field, would entice him like a moth to your flame. If he wasn't conscious and spiritually aware, he would think you were hot and approach you. You would talk and, with loosened inhibitions, he would at the least be siphoning off your vital energy. At the most, if you, too, were not energetically conscious, you might engage in some kind of sexual activity and you would pick up some of his messy and lower vibrational energy. In either case, whether you left it at flirting with loosened inhibitions or engaged in sexual activity, your vibration would be lower. That results in feeling tired, having low energy, feeling a little sad or grouchy (depression), and having lowered immune function (more susceptible to colds and other problems), body aches, even a less joyful outlook on life. Nobody wants that.

CONSCIOUS FLIRTING

So if you are going to go to a bar and drink alcohol, do it consciously. Drink minimally. Stay present. Own your space. Flirt with sober, high-vibrational dudes. Or wait to meet guys in less problematic settings such as at the bookstore, at the gym, while skiing, through friends, in spiritual workshops, at art gallery openings, at dance classes for single people, at poetry readings, in coffee houses. You get the idea.

In a clear environment where higher-vibe people gather and their energy isn't clouded by alcohol, such as in a book group, let's say you meet a man you find attractive and want to get to know better. How do you flirt with him consciously? You can smile and strike up a conversation about the particular book being signed. Yes, do a little well-executed hair toss or a playful wink across the room. If you are talking and his energy field feels good and clear, you can punctuate something you are saying by touching his arm. To read someone's field as high-vibe or not and tell whether it is clear, you need to use your instincts. Your intuition is already there inside of you and ready to roll. Notice your gut feelings, your first impressions. If you get the sense from a visceral place that someone is really kind, caring, and nice, they probably are. Follow up by observing. Do they act that way in all or most situations? To tell if someone is clear, notice their habits, too; do they smoke, drink alcohol much, need coffee daily? These substances all muddy up people's fields if used more than once or twice a week or in excess, with coffee/caffeine being the least severe. Trust your instincts and get your friends' first impressions too if they are around, and especially if they are intuitive types.

So to continue with you flirting with the guy with the clear energy in the bookstore. You just touched his arm to punctuate something you said. By breaking that physical barrier, you open the door to greater energy exchange. When the vibe is clear and positive, an energy exchange can be a great enhancement to life. A clean, happy, high-vibe person sharing a bit of energy with another high-vibe person is what interaction is meant to be. It fosters a feeling of connection and belonging in society. It's a demonstration of our interconnection with other people.

When you tap in for a quick energy exchange that a moment of physical contact provides, it will give you an idea of how he feels to you, intuitively, on a visceral level. Your intuition is your guide in flirting. It is instinctual.

Whose energy feels good, clean, positive? Do his words match his actions and your instinctive feel for him? Consciously noticing your intuition and your heart's response to a person can help you feel if it is right for you to flirt with him and how to do it. Does he respond to your energy, too? You can tell sometimes within the first thirty seconds of a meeting. It all shows up in your eyes and his. Take a quick look into his eyes. What do they say?

If a guy's words and actions don't match your instinctive feel for them, take notice. You meet someone and think he seems really mellow and kind—his vibe feels like that. But then you start to get to know him and his friends aren't mellow and kind. When he is around them he acts more like them. His words don't match the mellow and kind vibe. For example, he is watching a sporting event on television and bellows curse words and calls the players very crude derogatory names. Later, you hear him refer to a nosy coworker behind her back with those same words. Why don't his words match your initial impression of his vibe?

That could be a case of wanting to see something in him that is not there. We want to find the right guy, now. We are impatient and so sometimes we convince ourselves that someone is closer to our ideal than they really are. Just be very aware and listen to your instincts and then match them up with behaviors and words that show you your impressions in action.

WHAT NOT TO DO

Dee met someone on a spiritual dating site that she joined because there were not a lot of people to choose from in her area. The guy she met seemed cool. She agreed to meet him for coffee. She did not tell him where she lived. The meeting was fine. They talked; she talked more than he did. He was a math professor, which Dee related to because she was in a similar field as an accountant. Her instincts told her he was a little weird, but there was nothing specifically pinpointing his strangeness. He wasn't obviously rude or anything but he had a shaky vibe. His hands shook slightly sometimes, like a tremor. He was quiet but not in a shy way, rather in a way that was off somehow. Her instincts told her something didn't quite jibe. Dee should have looked at those clues at the time and noticed them more instead of brushing them off. Spiritual dating is about listening to your instincts and not rushing into anything.

He called and asked her out on a second date. She agreed, mostly because she was bored. This is a red flag on Dee's part. Spiritual daters don't go on second dates simply out of boredom.

They consider their sacredness and the other person's sacredness, whether they are spiritual or not, whether they are crazy nut jobs or regular Joes.

The life of an accountant was okay but most of her friends were married, some with children. Sometimes she got lonely for companionship. They went for dinner and she had a glass of wine; she wasn't a big drinker. A little buzzed, she decided to hang out more after dinner with him. Some more wine and she let him kiss her, just to see what it was like. It was not great. She left soon after. Dee went wrong here. Experimenting with physical and sexual expression opens an energetic door that is best left closed until you feel sure that the guy has a good vibe and that you really like him.

He asked her out on a third date. She went. Her intuition was starting to send warning signals, but her need to feel liked and attractive made her want to go on a date with someone, anyone, and feel admired and sought after. She knew something was off with him but again brushed her intuition aside. He was weird, and not in a good way; that was becoming obvious. What was really going on was that Dee needed the validation of men to feel attractive. She had been doing her spiritual work and mostly filling her own needs but she had yet to realize she was addicted to the accolades of men looking at her as beautiful.

She ignored that she was only excited about the prospect of a date, not at all about the guy. She ignored that she didn't really like him all that much. And mostly she ignored her intuition, which told her to stay away. She had decided it was fine to date for entertainment. After dinner, he kissed her in the parking lot. She left as quickly as possible and spit out the window repeatedly after she drove away. She realized that going on the date and especially kissing him was a bad idea. She didn't like this man. To be honest, she thought he was weird and a bit creepy. She didn't know what she had been thinking. Why would she have gone out with him again? She was just trying to be open-minded, hoping maybe she'd missed something positive about him. She hadn't.

That week he called and e-mailed her many times. She e-mailed back that she was not interested in continuing their relationship but wished him the best. He left a crazy message on her cell about being in love with her. Poems and lots of crazy behavior followed. This included repeated contact after she told him not to call or e-mail. She e-mailed again, more strongly, saying he was being creepy and not to contact her again ever. He kept calling. The calls and e-mails continued daily. Eventually she enlisted the police, who called him and told him he would be arrested for harassment if he continued to contact her. He stopped. Whew. It was pretty stressful for Dee. She felt as if she had to look over her shoulder all the time to make sure he wasn't following her. It was a terrible feeling.

She didn't behave consciously. This wasn't just flirting; it was more. Dee's boundaries were a mess in this situation. She let him kiss her when it was inappropriate. She agreed to additional dates when her instincts told her not to—and she didn't really like the guy. Her need for companionship led her to be unconscious and unkind. She didn't consider that someone she was not very serious about might be very serious about her.

If she had it all to do over again, she would not have seen him again after the first date. She would listen to her intuition, which quietly told her something was not right with him. If Dee had listened to her instincts, she would have saved herself a lot of hassle. Conscious behavior with appropriate boundaries is always the best choice. Trust Dee on this one.

TEST THE WATERS

Dating is all about compatibility. Ultimately, a romantic relationship requires two individuals who are compatible. Compatible doesn't necessarily mean "the same," though. Noticing compatibility early in the dating process will save you time and energy. It will also make the dating experience much more enjoyable. Compatibility means two people who can be together happily and peacefully and enhance each other's lives because of who they are. Shared values are often part of this. Shared interests are not a must but can enhance compatibility. Similar or harmonious emotional styles can make life together so much more pleasant and compatible, as when a person who is emotional and expressive partners with someone who is a calmer degree of emotional and expressive. This means they can understand each other and one calms the other and one brings the extra emotional passion.

POST-DATE COMPATIBILITY EXERCISE

Your intuition is going to show you whom you are compatible with. Tune into it. After a date, do this exercise. Keep a pen and paper handy to make notes if you would like.

1. Sit quietly in a meditative state. Clear your mind. Breathe deeply and evenly and relax into your seat or bed.

   • Bring your awareness into your heart center. Think of your date. Feel your heart. What does it tell you? How does it feel?
   • Now ponder the things you have learned so far in this book. How does your date fit with your dating desires and what you are looking for in a date or partner?

- Does he simply have potential you see or is his reality as great?
- Does he recognize your and his own sacredness?
- Are you spiritually aligned?
- Do you have similar values?

2. Do you feel a spark with him? Your body has a say in this, too.

3. Notice. Pay attention. Be aware of how you feel and also use your brain to look objectively at the potential relationship. Your compatibility or lack of it will be apparent before long. Listen to your heart first, your mind and spirit second, and then last but not least, and very importantly, your body. You are ready to successfully gauge your compatibility with your dates!

ONLINE DATING

Spiritual daters can use online dating sites to help them find dates. Some sites do a great job of gauging compatibility in terms of preferred gender, educational level, religious beliefs, previous marriages, and other basic information. However, you don't want to rule out people who might be right for you. For example, I had decided I wasn't interested in marrying a divorced man. The potential messiness with exes, especially if children were involved, was something I wanted to avoid. When I met my husband, I had no doubt at all that he was the one for me, and he felt the same way. He was divorced! I had to rethink my absolutes. By the same token, people on online dating sites sometimes misrepresent the facts about themselves. You may have to weed through fakers to find the real matches.

LILY GOES ONLINE

Lily was on the path of conscious and spiritual living. She was very into Buddhism and meditated daily. On an online spiritual dating site, she began communicating with Brent. He listed Buddhism as his religion, which she resonated with. They e-mailed back and forth and he seemed fine. Their e-mails were pretty generic in nature, but she agreed to talk on the phone to set up a meeting. When they talked, his voice didn't match her image of him according to his profile and e-mails. Her intuition alerted her to be aware. What was off, if anything? She decided to be ready to use her discernment.

Next, they met for coffee. His picture and his countenance were very different. He'd posted a picture from when he was much younger. His age was listed as thirty-six, but he looked to be in his fifties. Lily was thirty-five and was expecting someone her age. When she talked to him about his involvement in Buddhism, her intuition told her he was lying based on his vague answers and not making eye contact. She asked Brent straight out, "Are you even into Buddhism at all?"

He smirked, "Of course, of course." His eyes told another story.

Lily prepared to leave, getting her purse together and finishing her tea. Brent said, "Wait, wait. Okay, I'm not really into that spiritual stuff, but you are so hot, please come home with me. I haven't had sex in eight months!"

"So, let me get this straight—you aren't spiritual but you went on a spiritual dating site to find women to have sex with? Is that what is going on here?"

"Well, yeah, chicks who are into 'sexual exploration' are into the woo-woo stuff, I wanted to meet some ladies like that."

Lily walked out without another word. She was glad to have had her radar up right away and that she was able to detect Brent's B.S. on the first date. He didn't know where she lived or her home phone number, so she felt safe. He moved on to some other dating site soon enough. Lily was conscious and she approached online dating with her eyes wide open. She had faith that she would eventually find the right guy for her. Yes, she got irritated and frustrated with waiting. After Brent, she took a break from online dating, feeling it wasn't really working for her. Later that year she met a nice, spiritual man at a yoga retreat. He walked his talk. She got to see it for herself all weekend.

I believe that when the time is right people will find each other somehow, be it online or through some other avenue. And when the timing is not right, people find lessons, teachers, and karmically fueled dates (see Chapter 8 for more information about karmically fueled dates).

THE SPARK

The spark. The jolt of feel-good chemicals through the body. The thrill! It is so important. It has to be there for a relationship to prosper. That spark can really only be confirmed when you actually meet someone.

Remember Dee in the "What Not to Do" story earlier in this chapter? There was an example of potentially wasted time and energy. She spent quite a bit of time e-mailing the crazy guy before she met him. He didn't list in his online profile "prone to crazy, obsessive behavior." Would she have noticed it more quickly if she met him in person instead of online? Especially if she was already being conscious and spiritual about dating? She might have. It's hard to tell. But being conscious about dating extends to online dating too, that's for sure. Be aware of your flirting and energy exchanged, even online. Just because it is not in person, doesn't mean you don't need to be conscious.

Odette and Chris met online. They talked on the phone for months because they lived a few hours apart. When they finally met, there were no major sparks but they were both nice people with similar values. They dated consciously. When they did kiss, it was not for very long. Neither of them knew if they really felt "it." After five or so dates, they just fizzled into friends and then lost touch. They were both very glad that they took the physical relationship slowly. That is a main caveat about online dating: Let your intuition catch up with your friendship.

PRACTICE DATING

Practice dating is when you go on a date with someone that you do not feel is a potential long-term mate. You might not feel the spark of attraction with him. He may not be what you are looking for in a long-term partner. Practice dating gets you ready for the real thing when it arrives. Practice dating imparts social, romantic, and interpersonal skills and self-awareness in relationships. Lots can be learned by practice dating.

When you are dating, practice or not, being conscious means being kind. It means taking the other person's feelings into account. Are they practicing, too? You may not know that right away. So figure they are not. Make sure you are being authentic and kind when you practice date. Be truthful early on. If you don't feel that your connection is much more than friends but you think he is a wonderful man and you enjoy spending time together, tell him that.

Follow the advice from the "Flirting with Boundaries" section. Be aware of your energy and how you exchange it. Practice sacred, spiritual dating. Take things nice and slow and consider just being friends with most practice dates.

BEYOND PRACTICE DATING

Some women have dated a lot. They feel done with practice dating. They are ready for the real thing. If that is you, then it is time to be selective. Really go deep with your intuition. Practice using it. Notice how you intuitively feel with the waiter who serves your dinner, with your boss, with a cute guy you pass on the street. Replace practice dating with greater self-awareness and introspection. Do your emotional work.

USING YOUR INTUITION TO DECIDE WHETHER TO DATE SOMEONE

1. When an energy exchange occurs, pay attention. Notice your impressions, feelings. Do this with nondates first.

   - Notice what sense you get of a person you meet at a bookstore or somewhere neutral. Practice asking yourself for your first impression word. After you've met that person at the bookstore, when you walk away, ask yourself, "What is the first word that comes to mind when I free-associate about that person?"

   Deep?
   Quiet?
   Still?
   Happy?
   Pleasant?
   Love?
   Cutesy?
   Innocent?
   Secretive?

   - Next, when you meet a potential date—someone you find attractive and have talked to and who is about to ask you out or already has—ask yourself for the one word that describes him. Is it his essence?

2. How does it feel to your heart? Ask your heart: Does this resonate for me? Is it for my best to date this person?

Tune in to your first impressions and intuitive impulses. That means noticing the "little voice in your head." It means trusting your gut instincts and acting on that information and your feelings. Practice listening to your intuition in daily life to strengthen it for your dating life and beyond.

If you are coming back to dating after the end of a long-term relationship, you may find it hard to think about dating again. This is where practice dating can help. Eventually you will have to start dating again. Most likely, it is how you will find the partner you seek. But don't pressure yourself into thinking you have to find the right relationship now. There's no rush. Wait until you feel ready to date again. And then take it slowly. Any dating should be a conscious choice. Do it when it is fun and enhances your existence.

An important question is: what emotional space are you in? Are you ready to find your mate and get married? Have you been married and now are healed and seek a spiritual mate? With dating, what you are looking to find is important. If you know that, you'll be more equipped to know if you have found it.

The woman who has been dating for years and is ready to get married is in a different emotional space from the divorcée who has children and is reconnecting with her authentic self. In essence, if you are reading this book you are looking for a mate who is more than the conventional guy. He is spiritual or conscious. He wants to share a deep, fulfilling bond with you, not just get you pregnant, have you for companionship, and trot you out at work functions.

Figure out the specifics of your own emotional space. Do you need a kind, caring guy who can be there for you while you work through residual issues from past relationships? Do you want a man who wants to be a power couple with you? We are asking similar questions here about your intention. But we are asking them from your deep emotional space. What are you looking for in dates? Practice dates? The real thing? Know what you feel and use your heart to guide you.

CASUAL SEX: TO DO IT OR NOT TO DO IT, THAT IS THE QUESTION

Casual sex. Some women tell me it is sort of expected. In Manhattan, Meghan tells me, "By the third date, guys seem to think it is a sure thing. In fact, dates seem rare. There is a lot more 'hanging out' that goes on."

And one-night stands? "Super common. People are busy with work. A quick text and hookup are all lots of working men and women can be bothered with. I'm bored with it," Meghan shrugs.

How to navigate this is a question many women are asking themselves. If we believe the example of *Sex and the City*, casual sex is a normal part of single life. Even within relationships that last under six months, the sex is often casual—mostly for physical gratification.

SACRED SEX

When we have sex without love, some think we lose the essential goodness of the intimate act. Is the pleasure as intense? Does the afterglow last or is it replaced with regret or uncertainty?

As a woman, you are sacred. Sacred, in this book, is defined as perfection in body, your unique specialness, energy and matter combined in beauty. Sacred is not religious in this book. It is not judgmental. Sacredness loves and accepts you for who you are.

The real question is, does a potential casual sex act honor and respect your sacredness? Really, the question is, do you honor and respect your sacredness? Once you truly recognize how sacred you are, the next question to ask yourself about any potential partner is: does he (or she) recognize his or her sacredness and mine? And then, will this sex act or lovemaking fully honor us both and cause only benefit, no harm?

Most people who do see the sacredness of all life are on some kind of a conscious spiritual path. In seeing the beauty in all life, the act of intercourse becomes the sacred in each person honoring the sacred in the other person, in the spirit of unconditional love and ecstatic pleasure. If you can find this in the setting of casual sex, I'm impressed. It could happen. And occasionally, it does.

THE HEALING POWER OF SEX

Maryanne met Jim in massage school. He was a peripheral class-mate for a while and over time they became friends. Eventually, they traded massages outside of class and gave each other a chance to practice adding in their own healing techniques and energy work.

The healing work was emotional for Maryanne. She had left a difficult marriage earlier that year. She had a dream where she was told by an angel being that she would have healing sex. At the time, she never would have guessed it would be with Jim. But it was.

She describes how the essence of the divine feminine infused her, she felt it so palpably. Jim was asleep in her living room on the couch in a unexpected blizzard after a massage trade. From her bedroom, she felt him cold out there without enough blankets and got up to bring him more. She went to quietly place a fluffy blanket over him. He was awake. She allowed her instincts to guide her and asked if he wanted to come to her warm bed. He did.

Once in bed together, it felt new and different, she says, but somehow right in that moment. She knew Jim was not a compatible life-partner match. He lived five hours away on a co-op style, hippyish commune and Maryanne was a stylish, professional city girl. But the energy of unconditional love flowed between them, deeply loving and accepting and yet almost impersonal.

They kissed and caressed as more and more sacred energy flowed between them. She knew he respected her sacredness and his own. She knew his spiritual beliefs and she could feel them just from their kissing. At one point they stopped as she paused and tuned in to ask her body, mind, heart, and spirit if making love together would be right for her. She felt it was.

And so they did it. They made deep love, healing love. According to Maryanne, it was amazing. So pleasurable, so healing. She allowed the spirit of the sacred feminine to flow through her being and he allowed the spirit of the sacred masculine to flow through his. Some of her faith in love and pleasure was restored.

And that was it. He went home and they texted and talked. Both were content with that and cared for each other but more as friends. Over time they lost touch and casual but deeply loving sex was their memory of each other.

Maryanne and Jim had casual sex that wasn't really casual at all. It was love filled. Sacred. When we have love-filled sex that is clear and clean energetically, we are enhanced in all ways. When we have sex that is not love filled, we are negatively impacted energetically and emotionally. It is a fact. The energy body gets dented or heavy when nonlove energy is injected into it. The emotional body (made of energy, too) gets rubbed the wrong way. It gets roughed up as if some cosmic sandpaper abraded it, sometimes subtly, sometimes obviously. The obvious emotional sandpaper effect is crying and feelings of discontent and shame. The subtle effect is slightly feeling something is off. Sometimes we don't consciously notice the effect, but it is there, eroding our energy body and emotional health.

Casual sex is best done with a loving, conscious, spiritual partner under very special and rare circumstances.

CASUAL AND SACRED SEX	
Casual Sex	Sacred Sex
impersonal	honoring
using each other	loving each other
breeds uncertainty	communicating with love
feelings of insecurity	unconditional acceptance
energetic sandpaper	love energy bath
emotionally abrasive	emotionally pleasurable
feels wrong	spiritually aligned
damages aura	enhances vital life force

WHEN IT IS REAL

The question is often, how do you know when it is real? It: the true love, the deep connection, the bond that outshines all the rest. Many couples who are deeply in love and happy often say, "We just knew. 'It' was undeniable." It is true. When all factors are aligned and both people are ready, you do just know, totally, unequivocally you know, in your bones. If there is any question, then it is a no.

Many people settle for less than a total completely certain yes and are relatively happily married. Some of these people really wanted children and a family. Some were tired of being alone; they craved companionship. Some are content with what they have and that is wonderful.

You have to decide what you want. If you want nothing less than glorious, massive, true love with your spiritual soul mate and are prepared to not settle for anything less, then when that soul mate comes, you will know. When everything aligns, suddenly there is no question. You deeply want to be with that person and you know that it is great for you. It enhances your life and his. It is the real thing. Your body knows. Your heart knows. Your mind knows, too, because this person makes sense in your life. Your spirit knows it has found a kindred. Your soul glories in the love between you. He feels the same way—total unconditional love and acceptance.

Questions fly out the window for you both. You will work out the crazy in-laws or the geographic distance or the religious differences. You just must be together and it is mostly easy. Anything less than that is not the complete spiritual, sacred, real thing. And that is okay. But for those who want it, know that "almost" is not it and the real thing is out there. Have faith and be in love with yourself. Make space in your life for the real thing. Time will bring you the real thing when you least expect it. Ready your being and get your emotional and mental house in order. 'Cause you are wonderful!

Part Four

Keep Your Third Eye Wide Open

The more conscious you are, the more you realize the importance of awareness. We talked in earlier chapters about being aware of your sexual energy and conscious of how you are directing it while flirting and on dates. In the early phases of dating, it is so crucial to be aware. Be aware of how your date interacts with you and others. Is he respectful and kind? How he presents himself can tell you a lot about him, too. How does he dress for a first date? How does he act? Pay attention to your instincts! Use your intuition, your heart, and your brain to discern whether he is a good date for you. You can save yourself lots of time and potential heartbreak by keeping your third eye wide open. Your third eye is the energy center located in the middle of your forehead and between your physical eyes. It houses your ability to "see" in an extrasensory way. It governs your intuition along with your heart and especially your "gut." In Part 4, we discuss awareness in all of its aspects, including recognizing and dealing with other people's energy and learning how to be impervious to it. We look deeply, with women's stories, at the choices we make in our relationships and how to choose most healthfully for ourselves. This level of awareness makes our dating lives so much richer and easier.

Clearing away dense energies and being aware of energetic predators is illuminated, too. We work through many important spiritual dating concepts and experiences to ultimately better your life through conscious, aware choices. Although you'll discover there's a lot to know about this topic, spending time to develop your awareness will help you continue to transform your dating life into a sacred expression of your joy and happiness.

Chapter Seven
Unconscious Dating Affects Your Life

Our lives are supremely affected by the men we date and are intimate with. Not only do our energies exchange and intertwine with our dates (as we discussed in Chapter 6), we also spend significant amounts of our time with people we date repeatedly—which means we take in parts of their worldview. We might listen to their advice and opinions and hear their comments and judgments about ourselves and others in what might be a negative way. When people spend lots of time together, they adapt, become more like each other.

Most importantly, we exchange lots of energy and vital life force with them. That is why it is best to be conscious and mindful of our sacredness in our dating life. Unconscious dating behavior can have damaging effects. We might mix our energy with someone whose energy is negative and lowers our vibration. We might listen to a date's advice only to make a wrong decision at work and have more difficulty there. We might be intimate with someone, against our intuition's warning, only to contract an STD. Sometimes we are cleaning up our unconscious dating messes for years afterward. For example, this could be paying off credit card debt we incurred trying to look the way our partner wanted or being emotionally devastated by our partner's verbal or physical abuse.

If we respect ourselves and our sacredness, we must be conscious daters. We have to cultivate consciousness and awareness. We need to remain aware and present, not drunk or ungrounded, when we date new people. In time, when we get to know someone and feel our values are aligned with his and we can trust our dating partner, then we can relax and open ourselves up. We can show our vulnerability in increments in an emotionally mature manner. In this way, we can gauge where our dating partners can meet us in terms of emotional maturity.

- Be authentic about who you are. For example, if you meet someone online, be honest about who you are—a divorced mom, a career woman in her forties who has never been married—but also be cautious and do not give out your home address or number until you have gotten to know him well. You don't lie about being on antidepressants, but wait until you feel comfortable and know he won't have a Tom Cruise moment to tell him. If it does come up and he has a Tom Cruise moment, then you know that there is a major compatibility issue there and you probably should move on, unless a lot of emotionally mature communication happens about it.
- A man's attitude about past relationships can show you a lot about his emotional maturity. If he talks about his ex using swear words or lots of negative talk, it probably indicates a lack of emotional maturity.
- Be real, yourself, yet safe in all ways. Emotionally, reveal yourself in increments that are congruent with your comfort level. Take the time to get to know your date and know that an emotionally mature guy will do the same.

Definitions of Lovemaking Terms

In this chapter, we'll be talking about the impact sexual intercourse has on you emotionally, spiritually, even financially. So, let's define some terms for clarity.

- **Intercourse:** When a man's penis is inserted into a woman's vagina or the equivalent act for lesbian/gay couples.
- **Sex:** Intercourse plus any acts of foreplay.
- **Lovemaking:** Sex plus love, loving feelings, and love energy flowing between both parties.
- **Sacred Lovemaking:** Lovemaking plus a deep spiritual connection between partners (most often monogamous and committed to each other). Heart centered and deeply honoring.
- **Sacred Marriage Lovemaking:** Sacred Lovemaking that occurs between married or life-partnered couples and is done with specific healing and uplifting intentions set by the couple.

The heart is our main energy center for attracting what we want from life. The heart is our magnet. When we involve clear, pure love in our intentions to attract what we want and need, we amplify those requests to the universe manyfold.

When we date unconsciously, our emotional energy bodies can be impacted. We exchange energy with our dates and with everyone we spend time with. So if our dates are not a high-vibrational, kind, clear match for us, than we may pick up some of their less healthy energy. We can also put ourselves in situations that are ultimately not for our highest good—such as too much wine and a make-out session with a guy who is not energetically clear or good for us. Or a relationship where the guy is less into us than we are him and ultimately our expectations are not met and we are disappointed.

With discernment and awareness, we can see things we were previously blind to, such as how a date is not a good partner for us. We probably all have stories of willful blindness. When you are dating unconsciously, you may make excuses for a guy's wandering eye. You tell yourself that all guys do that. But when you are dating spiritually, you know you deserve better than a guy who is always checking out other women and you are not afraid that this is as good as dating is going to get.

The stories ahead in this chapter are reminders of how unconscious dating and unconscious sex affect our lives. They can help you integrate any similar past relationships you may have experienced and avoid creating any of these scenarios for yourself in the future.

INTERCOURSE, DATING, AND YOUR FINANCIAL ABUNDANCE

Let's be real. Sex is a man's penis, *a part of his body*, going *inside* of your body for a sometimes extended (and sometimes not!) period of time. Everything that is on or around that penis is going inside of you. Energy, skin cells, sweat, stored emotions, and any beliefs housed in those cells of the body. Everything.

Energetically speaking, sex is very powerful—for good or bad. Consider how the chakra system works. Chakras are energy centers spread evenly throughout our bodies. Our reproductive organs lie in the middle of our first and second chakras (the first chakra is located at the base of our spine and the second is all around our belly button area all the way through to our back). The first chakra governs our survival, our drive to live and acquire everything that sustains us. The second chakra holds the energy of our instincts, our sexual desire, our sensuality, and—this may be somewhat surprising—our financial ideals. It presides over our abundance energy, which is the energetic magnetism that draws money (among other things) to us.

The second chakra is also the seat of the emotional body. The layer of energy surrounding our physical body is called our emotional body. It houses the energy of our feelings and emotional experiences. Anything you haven't worked through emotionally from your past or present echoes through that field and can sometimes be transferred and intermingled through sex when you are intimate with someone you are physically and psychically close to. There is no getting around that fact. As we press our bodies together, energies get mixed. It is inevitable. Our sexual partner's thought-forms and beliefs about money can leak into our field of energy and vice versa. It is not a matter of being suggestible or weak-minded; it is just the biology of energy.

Our money-magnetism needs to be—and needs to *stay*—strong and clear. It is how we sustain ourselves and meet our material needs. Envision your "money magnet" like a resonant form in your lower belly; it draws money to it. To you. What does yours look like? It might look like a ball of vital energy. It might be a color or might be clear. It might be in the shape of something; if it is, it should be something healthy and pleasant, such as a geometric shape or a dollar sign.

If you are sexually active, you need to be aware that your partner's energy field is going to affect yours in some way. To keep your internal energetic money magnets strong and clear, you need to be very mindful of whom you are intimate with. To be sure that a date is not negatively affecting your money magnet, you should know him well and know that he is kind, caring, clear, and loving; that he doesn't have money issues of his own (within reason and taking into account a lousy job market); that he is honest, positive, heartfelt.

Do not take sex lightly. Be conscious of your well-being and sacredness. To begin, keep your field clear and highly vibrational. Joy is a good byword for our sex lives. Do you feel joyful and expansive with your partner? Is the general mood positive? How does his energy field feel? Clear? High-vibe? Joy-filled? Affluent? Take notice. It really affects your life!

The stories below illustrate some examples of women whose sex lives affected their pocketbooks directly. Awareness is the key here. As we discussed in Chapter 6, casual sex can be a detriment to your energy body; this is true of your money-magnetism, too. As you read the examples below, do any of them sound familiar? Has your pocketbook been affected by your sex life in the past? Think about how to avoid that in the future.

STORIES OF FINANCES AFFECTED BY SEXUAL ENERGY

The stories below mostly detail experiences of women who lived with the men in their lives. The energetic effect on their financial abundance became very obvious at the end of their relationships. But the problems started the very first time these women were intimate with these men. Their energy bodies were affected for a long time and the repeated sex with the men in question further exacerbated the mentality of lack, or poverty, or lowered self-esteem. Read on and see what you do not want to become. If instead you are aware of the way sex affects your financial and emotional energy, then you can make good dating choices that only enhance your well-being and you will know what to do if you encounter a man you would be better off without.

RIGID AND SCARED

Catlyn dated Checkov, a man from a very patriarchal society in Europe. In his culture, the man provided and the woman was subservient to him. This couple had financial and relationship difficulties often. From the beginning this man did not support Catlyn or enhance her self-esteem. After they had been dating for a few weeks, he told her she was too loud, too exuberant. He wanted her to be quieter, more passive, not herself. The vibe in their home and relationship became very melancholy and they were not energized or happy.

Checkov was laid off. After that he had a failed business. Everything got worse. His belief that his worth was tied to bringing in the money was transferred to Catlyn via intercourse, and because he was not bringing home any money the energy was very negative. She was physically ill and worked at a menial, minimum-wage job even though she was college educated and had trained to be a nurse practitioner. Her self-esteem plummeted and she put on weight. She eventually sought treatment for depression.

Her partner was deeply rigid, which was due partially to his upbringing and partially to his personality. He was scared and felt worthless so he acted out. He became cruel and unappreciative. He was unkind to her and called her names when he was feeling particularly bad about himself.

Upon leaving the relationship, Catlyn had some emotional rebuilding to do. She divorced her husband and went back to work as a nurse practitioner. She sought counseling with a gentle female psychologist. Two years later and fifty pounds lighter, she says she feels financially secure and abundant and is ready to love and be loved by an emotionally healthy and loving partner. Putting an end to the physical, sexual merging with her ex-husband's energy allowed her to tap back into her own wellspring of joy and self-esteem and she feels happier and more stable now.

PAPA WAS A ROLLING STONE

Milly was psychically sensitive and extremely intuitive. She could communicate with animals and later in life would be called to do that professionally. At twenty-one, she met Jim. It was love at first sight. The feelings were strong and the pheromones even stronger. Some time went by and the couple decided to move in together. Jim's poor financial habits quickly took center stage. As a construction worker, his job was weather dependent, plus he had a pattern of not showing up to work if the surf was up, regardless of the weather.

Milly began to pay most of the bills with money from her medical assistant job. Resentment bloomed but she swept it under the rug. Jim resented Milly's work ethic, something he did not have the drive to sustain. Milly resented Jim's lack of financial contribution to their lifestyle. When Milly met Jim's dad, things began to make sense—but in some ways she was more confused. Jim's dad was an alcoholic who no longer drank. He was heavily involved with Alcoholics Anonymous. But the key point that Milly noticed was that he lied—all the time.

She asked Jim about the lying. He said that his dad had always been that way. He lied to their mom during the marriage and after the divorce. Sometimes he would take the kids to the bar on his visits with them and leave them to their own devices, then later lie about it to their mom. Sometimes he would just not show up for his visits with the kids. Jim rationalized that things were better because the drinking was not happening.

Jim held the energy of inconsistency and unreliability in his first and second chakra. He was raised with an example of it and he chose to continue some of those patterns. After the relationship ended, Milly found out from mutual friends that Jim had lied to her frequently and slept around during the relationship. Although devastated, she was not particularly surprised.

When Milly and Jim split, things began to change for Milly. She first needed to clear the psychic and emotional energy from years of having Jim's penis inside of her body. There was a residue. She did that with a variety of forms of energy-cleansing on her own and with several practitioners. Forms of energy-cleansing include smudging with sage, using sound such as a drum or loud chime all around the body, seeing an acupuncturist who specializes in clearing energy, or consulting with a shaman or a medical intuitive. As that energy cleared, Milly got a raise at her job and began to consult as an animal communicator on the side. She began to trust herself to help others and it showed in her confidence level. Pretty quickly, her animal communication business was thriving and kept her happily busy full time.

Her income and happiness level grew exponentially. Years later she discovered a bill that Jim had lied about paying, which was in her name, that went into collections and created a small blemish on her credit report. But her life had improved drastically and this didn't affect her at all.

LOOK IN THE RELATIONSHIP MIRROR

When we choose to date people who are not so good for us, often it's because they mirror certain parts of us. You can integrate those aspects of your being and eliminate the need to attract more mirrors like that in your life. For example, after her relationship with Jim ended, Milly processed the under-the-surface parts of herself that are unreliable and inconsistent. Her honesty with herself helped her reap the lessons from her experience and move forward with no spiritual reason to recreate it again. She integrated and honored the mirrored parts of herself and she was done! They exist. She accepts them.

To understand how the weaknesses, problems, and issues of the men you dated in the past mirror your own weaknesses, problems, and issues, take some time to dig past your surface self. Ask these questions to get started:

- What have past dates or boyfriends mirrored for you? To figure this out, notice what bothered you about them. If someone was a cheater and a liar, notice how although you may not cheat or lie, you may feel dishonest somewhere inside of you. Acknowledge that. See if you can remedy that and integrate it. Foster your own integrity.
- Are there parts of yourself that you judge as bad or feel ashamed of? If yes, you must get over that. We are all everything! Yes, a part of you might be slightly out of integrity, even if just in a thought. Accept yourself.
- What are these parts you judge or feel ashamed of?
- Can you honor and integrate them and yet notice how you do not live them frequently?
- Can you accept those parts of yourself?

THE GOOD NEWS

Lovemaking can positively influence our financial abundance as well. This is great news!

Experiences of lovemaking (see the sidebar "Definitions of Lovemaking Terms" earlier in the chapter) have the potential to improve our energetic lives on the whole and our financial energetic blueprint. When both partners have dealt with most of their energetic issues and have clean, clear first and second chakras and overall energy fields, their lives and bodies have the potential to be enhanced by lovemaking.

Sacred Lovemaking has even more potential to enhance our lives. With spiritual energy and connection flowing through us as we make love, we are amplified by universal life force and spiritual oneness. We may experience transcendence in our lovemaking. This is healing for body, mind, heart, and spirit, which in turn heals our money-attracting energetic vibration (our money magnet in our abdomen and our heart magnet in the center of our chest).

Sacred Marriage Lovemaking has the most potential to better our existence. With the safety of a lifelong bond, we can deeply explore the energies and intentions we focus on as a couple. Trust and commitment are sexy! We can experience ecstatic oneness and deep love with our partner and our Source/Divinity.

Intentions that we set for healing and abundance can be transmitted to the universe amid a massive vibration of ecstatic energy through Sacred Marriage Lovemaking. Think of the powerful vibration we send out this way. Now carry that through to the powerful results that energy can yield.

BE YOUR OWN SEXUAL PARTNER

Generally, it is energetically and emotionally better to be without a sexual partner than to be with one there are issues with, as is evidenced by the two stories shared earlier in the chapter. But being without a sexual partner is impossible if you look at it from the standpoint that you are one of your own best sexual partners. Who better to satisfy and love you than you?

To bring the energy of abundance home to your body, I recommend several important steps.

STEP 1
Clear your energy field of past sexual partners' energetic residues.

1. Soak in sea salt baths. This clears electrical energy that is out of balance from your body and the energy field surrounding it.

2. "Smudge" your auric field (your body's energy bubble surrounding you) by safely burning a fragrant herb such as sage and wafting it all around your body. Imagine that the smoke is whisking away all dense and heavy energy that has ever been in your auric field.

3. Write down the names of your sexual partners and any angering or saddening experiences surrounding your sexuality, and then burn the list in a safe manner.

4. You can use the Violet Flame energy-cleansing process (see the sidebar in Chapter 2) to clear past partners' residues.

Finally, disconnect from all past sexual partners' energies for all time. Do this by stating the following aloud with intention: 'I now disconnect from _____ (list all partner's names or say 'all of my sexual partners') for all time in all dimensions, all interdimensions, and all realities as needed for my highest good and the highest good of all life. I release all energies associated with these sexual relationships from my life and being in the spirit of gratitude and ask that they be released from my focus for all time. It is done."

STEP 2

If you do not already have one, begin a loving sexual and/or sensual relationship with yourself. Brainstorm all the ways you would love for a partner to treat you: flowers, bubble baths, gentle sensual lovemaking, supportive words and phrases of encouragement and tender gestures, nature walks, whatever makes you feel loved and treasured. Now start doing these things for yourself. Commit to doing one of your brainstormed actions twice or more a week. Schedule it if you need to. Feeling loved and treasured comes first. Then sensual and sexual pleasure can follow as you feel safe and in the mood.

STEP 3

Making love to yourself can be done with the same healing and abundance-infused intention as with a partner. State your intention and place your hand on your heart center beforehand and really tap into the love energy in your heart as you open to its spiritual essence. Then continue the self-lovemaking process as you choose. Give yourself time for sexual pleasure, just as you would in a relationship, just as you might set aside time for romancing yourself in Step 2.

Healing ideas are further shared in Chapter 10 and include repeating positive loving affirmations while experiencing sexual pleasure, such as "I am love"; "I am sacred"; "I honor my sacred, loving sexuality"; "I am pure love-light."

If fantasizing, imagine you are with your soul mate. Feel how the experience would also be full of love.

CONSCIOUS DATING ENHANCES YOUR LIFE

When you give your mind, body, and heart the message that you are worth the effort of being conscious, miraculous things start to happen. Your health and vitality often improve. Imagine how happy your being can become when you are conscious and when your outlook is focused on the sacred in yourself and in others. Your life transforms on deep, obvious, and subtle levels. This happens because you act differently and make different choices, and also because your physical cells are made to feel sacred. When they do, your health and well-being are enhanced.

Dating consciously gives your heart the message that you get it, your heart is sacred, precious, important, worthy of care. It is a revelation. Everything restructures emotionally around that new fact. The heart can almost be heard saying, "I am sacred. I am known now. I am recognized for my truth. I can start to relax and feel safe." You are that safety. You provide it.

Dating from the place of internal emotional safety tells your being that you will care for it well. You will provide tender care for your sacred self. You will make choices that honor your heart and body. How relaxing to know that you are trustworthy with your own well-being, mind, body, heart, soul, and spirit!

Can you be that caring, nurturing self who recognizes your sacredness? Can you apply that knowledge and action to each date? I think you can. A bit of change may be required, whether in attitude or action, but you are a capable steward of your body, caretaker of your heart, supporter of your mind, and nurturer of your spirit. Go forth with confidence in your ability as a sacred steward of your being. You can do it!

Chapter Eight
How to Date Consciously

As a conscious dater, you need to be aware of factors beyond the physical that contribute to the quality of your dating experiences. As we've discussed in previous chapters, currents of energy or vital life force flow all around us all of the time. When we talk with someone, we exchange energy. When we share time with someone, we exchange energy proportionate to how much we bond and how open we are. On dates, we are constantly exchanging energy. How much and whether it is enhancing or detrimental can vary. Energy exchange is the essence of our interaction with people, animals, and plants. Think of how some people lift you up and enliven your life with their presence. These people enhance your life.

On the other hand, some people make you feel tired, drained, or slightly out of sorts after you spend time with them. These are people to be aware of; modulate the amount of time you spend with them. If you are considering dating someone who makes you feel this way, think twice. Is it in your best interest to spend lots of time with someone who drains you? Especially potentially intimate time?

The dating buzzword of this chapter is *awareness*. Be aware of your patterns and tendencies, and your partner's energetic vibe. You are respecting your sacredness when you make the best choices for your health and well-being in concert with being aware.

IDENTIFY YOUR DATING RED FLAGS

Red flags are warning signals that our brains use to tell us to pay attention. They pop up when our intuition and/or intellect and/or heart knows that something is not right. An example is when a person we are dating repeatedly does something slightly off, such as breaking dates at the last minute or overdrinking and misbehaving. Our bodies and brains respond to this by trying to alert us using a red-flag signal.

A red-flag signal is usually a knowing feeling. A part of us just knows something is off. We feel that something is not right. Sometimes we ignore red flags or talk ourselves out of them. We want to believe the best about people, especially people we care about.

In this chapter, we endeavor to identify past red flags and how our body, in particular, alerts us, so we can listen and heed our intuition and knowing in future situations.

WAYS YOUR BODY TELLS YOU SOMETHING IS OFF

Here are some ways you might get a body signal that a red flag has come up:

- Feeling sick to your stomach
- Developing tension in your body, neck, and shoulders
- Feeling slightly out of your body
- Feeling restless
- Averting your eyes, as if you do not want to see the red flag
- Sensing uneasiness creeping up your spine

RED FLAGS QUIZ

1. Think about when you have had a gut feeling. Remember a specific instance when that occurred. What did it feel like? Did you feel it in your body? Did your breathing change? Write about this in your journal or on a separate sheet of paper.
2. Next, think of your most unhealthy relationship. Look back at the first instance when something was evidenced to be wrong. Reimagine it.

   - How did you feel emotionally?
   - How did you feel physically? Jamie's red-flag-signal moments grew in scope as her body tried to get her attention. They culminated when she tried to have sex with her then boyfriend and broke out in full body hives. Her body took over and yelled, shouted, "Do not have sex with him!" She found out later that he had cheated with a coworker the day before and had had unprotected sex.
   - How did you feel psychically or mentally? Did you think something was off? Did you feel a quick sense of foreboding?
   - Did you feel disrespected?
   - Did you heed any of these feelings or push them under the rug for later? Don't judge yourself, either way. Simply notice.
   - What was your body's way of throwing up a red flag in that relationship?
   - Did you get your red-flag signal(s) more than once during that relationship?

3. Have you gotten red-flag signals during other relationships? How long did it take you to heed them?
4. Have you felt your red-flag signals during a current relationship?

Use the self-knowledge you uncover while reading this chapter to be aware of red flags as they arise. Value yourself enough to act on the signals your body sends. When we learn all we need from past relationships, we eliminate the need to create the same lessons with new people. Red flags are our allies! Be grateful for them!

As you date and meet potential dates, keep your red-flag triggers in mind. Keep alert to your body's signals. What does your gut tell you? Listen to your intuition and red-flag signals. Date with awareness.

UNCONSCIOUS CHILDHOOD AND PAST RELATIONSHIP PATTERNS

Sometimes our unconscious does the date choosing for us. When that happens, strife often does, too. Any unresolved issues we have with our paternal authority figures can come into play. As women dating men, if we have habitual patterns about the way we reacted and interacted with our fathers or fatherlike figures that we have not fully resolved, they create a big, easily pushable button for our dates.

Here is an example: Let's say a woman had a childhood issue where she felt that her father didn't prioritize her as an important part of his life. She felt that something else was always more important than she was. She may not have even put words to this situation as a child; she may have just felt lacking emotionally.

If she does not deal with and work through these issues, she will have the propensity to relive this pattern in her romantic relationships. That could play out with her feeling and acting as if she had to corral her dates and relationship mates into spending time with her. She would always feel that her dates were trying to get out of it. The funny thing is, she would attract dates and partners who would do exactly that! It is a weird phenomenon of the magnetic attraction of people. Because she hadn't dealt with that issue, she would attract the very men who would push that button by not wanting to spend time with her when she was a great date and girlfriend that most men would want to spend time with.

Instead of doing that—dating unconsciously—she could choose to work through those issues. She could do whatever she needed to do, be it psychotherapy, journaling, anything, to give herself the clear message that people want to spend time with her, especially men, especially her dates. By doing this she would literally change the types of dates she attracts and chooses to go out with. It is pretty amazing, really.

Think about how this might apply to you.

- Was your dad too overprotective, so you attract possessive men who inadvertently give you the message that you are helpless?
- Did your dad humiliate you in public, so now you attract dates who do the same but in different ways?
- Was your dad obsessed with appearances and putting on the facade of a close family in public, so now you attract inauthentic guys who are only affectionate in public?
- Did your dad leave when you were a baby, so now you attract emotionally unavailable men with commitment issues?

Do not discount maternal issues in this equation, too. The same concept applies to unresolved issues we have with our mothers. An example is an overbearing mother who was a taskmaster. You may either unconsciously attract that kind of partner or unconsciously become similar to that with a passive partner, acting out the old pattern. A mother who simply sent you outside to play with very little physical affection or warmth ever given might inspire a daughter who feels the need to control all situations to avoid feeling hurt or a daughter who is supremely passive and feels unworthy. These women might attract partners who (in the case of the controller) are not their equals or who (in the case of the passive woman) walk all over them.

Most of our parental issues are fueled by not feeling as loved as we needed to feel. Children are open, raw, and ready for the deepest love connection, and lack the walls to this that life builds. They are wired to crave real, true, authentic love, and their parents are the people in the best position to give them that. Kids need that love for their emotional survival. Most of our parents tried their best, but sometimes people are not emotionally equipped for the stresses and challenges of raising children while making a living and functioning in society.

The key to not reenacting our childhood issues is to resolve them by giving ourselves the love and emotional support we felt we were lacking as children. We still crave this love; it is an unfulfilled need, until we fulfill it. So how can you fill your particular unfulfilled needs?

FULFILLING YOUR UNFULFILLED CHILDHOOD NEEDS

To fulfill your unfulfilled childhood needs is a process that requires you to dig deep into what happened in your childhood and to figure out ways you can give yourself what was missing.

1. Give this some real time and go into your heart and ask it, in its childhood forms, what it needs. Get into a meditative state and bring your awareness to your heart. Go into it for this exercise. You can keep a journal handy and work this out with some writing and free-associating, too.

2. What does your heart crave? How does it want its love served up? As children, we probably couldn't name these needs. See if you can put a name to what feels like it is missing in your heart from way back then. Go deeply into your heart and allow yourself to feel these unmet needs.

3. Then provide those needs for yourself. Become your own love supplier. If your childhood lacked fun, figure out what would be super-fun for you, be it a trip to an amusement park or a Zumba dance class. If your childhood was fraught with worry over where your next meal would come from and devoid of love and affection, then you need to give yourself a feeling of abundance of everything good: love, resources, all of your needs abundantly met. For that, you might create an affirmation such as, "I am infinitely supplied with all I need and desire. Everything is provided for me with love! I believe in love and my ability to receive its abundance." In addition, you could think of some ways to love yourself in an abundant and warm way, such as sending yourself an extravagant bouquet or treating yourself to a loving and thoughtful evening of your favorite foods and an upbeat romantic comedy.

Keep on top of this and continue to be aware of it even when it is mostly resolved and you are in a healthy relationship. Keep loving yourself in the unique way you need to. If buttons get pushed, use them as tools for awareness; love yourself more and figure out what unmet need you need to fill. In some ways this is a lifelong process, but you can make great progress now. It may occasionally come up in the future in new ways, such as wanting your partner to pay complete attention when you are talking and not multitask if you felt unheard as a child. Or feeling a little unnerved when a partner occasionally goes out of town for work if you had a parent who was not there very much. But you will know what to do about it. Just fulfill those needs as they come up.

KARMIC DATE FUEL VERSUS TRUE CONNECTION

After a date or even an entire relationship, have you ever wondered "What was I thinking?" Sometimes the answer is, you weren't. Other factors were at play. These could be old familial patterns, chemical attraction that caused temporary poor judgment, red flags that were ignored, or, sometimes, karma.

Talk of karma generally refers to past lives, lives that our souls have experienced other than this one. I want to expand the definition for our purposes. Over eleven years of spiritual counseling and medical intuitive work, I have noticed that sometimes karma is very specific for people—it directly affects their lives—and sometimes it is more general—the collective energy of all of the people who have ever lived on Earth contributing to people's lives and situations. That second definition speaks more to the Jungian concept of the "collective unconscious," a concept that tells us that all of our minds and hearts are connected in some way because we share a collective human unconscious in addition to our own individual subconscious. Our world is a world of interconnection.

Interconnection can be like what Obi Wan said in *Star Wars*, prior to finding out the entire planet of Alderaan was blown up: "I felt a great disturbance in the Force, as if millions of voices suddenly cried out in terror and were suddenly silenced. I fear something terrible has happened." You don't have to be a Jedi to feel interconnection. I believe that that ability is already wired into our bodies. Some people call it intuition or gut-knowing. Some call it the collective unconscious.

In Holly and Nicholas's story below, you'll see how people's relationships can continue throughout several lives. If you don't believe in reincarnation, you can also look at this story as allegorical or metaphorical. What really matters is healing for the people involved and awareness of factors that may be influencing who we date and why.

As spiritual and conscious women, we can choose to be aware of karmic date fuel and recognize it. We will work on clearing our relationship karma later in the chapter. If we are aware and consciously evolving through our karma, we can choose true connection that is not based on karma. In that way, we can find the right partners who are best for us.

PHARAOH'S SEED

Holly came to me after a tough breakup. She had dated Nicholas for over three years. They lived together for awhile rather inharmoniously. He was a partier and she wasn't.

After things had been going downhill emotionally for a while, she came home one night after a long workday to her lovely house filled with beer cans, ashes, and mostly dudes. She and Nicholas had already discussed not having parties in the house without both agreeing first, so she was livid. She told him in private to clear the people out. She was tired and had to work early the next morning. He refused and went out to rejoin the party.

She hid in their bedroom and locked the door. Eventually she had to come out to use the restroom. She went into the full bath to find the very strong odor of beer and an empty beer can. She leaned into the shelf where she neatly rolled the towels; they were covered in beer and were too high up to have been accidentally spilled on. Someone deliberately poured beer on them. She knew intuitively who it was, one of Nicholas's especially sleazy friends.

She was done. She went back to the bedroom and called the local police. She explained the situation. The cops came and broke up the party. She kicked Nicholas out at the same time, while the cops were there. They stayed and made sure he was gone. She owned the house and had spent years saving the down payment and caring for it. She figuratively woke up that night. Nicholas clearly did not respect her or the house she was letting him live in. He was out and that was all.

When she came to me, we tapped into her spiritual energy and asked for whatever healing was needed for her to move on from the relationship because she was having a hard time emotionally. She said she didn't understand what motivated her to stay in the relationship so long. It was apparent early on that their two lifestyles were way too divergent. When she first met Nicholas, his wild side attracted her. He was fun and social. The luster wore off once they were together for about six months.

As for spiritual healing, what came up for her was a life where she lived in a society like that of ancient Egypt. She was a pharaoh there, a king. This pharaoh loved his queen very much. She was light and ethereal. She had a delicate constitution and was very beautiful according to the standards of the time and place.

The queen worried when he went off to battle, which was often. When the pharaoh was off in the country, it was his job to sow the royal seed. He was supposed to demonstrate virility for the health of the crops and his people. It was accepted, and even expected, for him to sow his seed in as many women as possible. The queen was passive and although it saddened her, she did nothing.

As we said, in this story Holly lived as the pharaoh, or at the very least identified with him deeply via the collective unconscious. Nicholas was the queen. In that life, they loved each other very much but there were issues born of the customs of the society.

Holly integrated and worked through the scenario. She wove the good parts into her body's energetic matrix and let the rest go. She saw how the past life provided the karmic fuel that attracted her to Nicholas and how when the karmic fuel wore off, so did her feelings.

In a phone call, months later, she revealed some new and, to her, unexpected news. She had run into a friend who knew Nicholas. He told her that Nicholas had been sleeping with many different women at house parties Holly did not attend during their relationship. The friend was very glad she was rid of Nicholas and told her she deserved more than that.

Holly said in a way she was shocked and in a way not surprised. His behavior sometimes tended toward the erratic and she'd caught him in several lies over the years. In light of the experience that they had in their Egyptian-like life, she could also see how their karma was trying to balance. When it did, the attraction to each other evaporated completely.

It is important to note that relationships are an inefficient way of working through karma. As a spiritual, conscious woman who recognizes your sacredness, you can do it another way. I'll teach you how.

HOW TO BALANCE YOUR RELATIONSHIP KARMA

Balancing your relationship karma will help your love life in myriad ways. You will attract dates who are not there simply to balance karma; instead they will be there because of real, true connection. Your dating life will come into greater alignment with the sacred and it will be lighter and more fun. It will be a very positive change! Do it!

Part of balancing karma is accepting that it exists. When you can feel okay about the fact that you are part of everything and that, in the case of karma, you have been everything—lover, fighter, queen, serf, killer, saint—then you are ready to balance karma consciously.

See if you can feel this concept viscerally: You have been all things. You have been the saint. You have been the tyrant. You have been the submissive child. You have been the oppressor. You are part of everything and everything is sacred. Accepting the sacredness of all life is part of integrating the depth of our human experience. Sometimes it is especially hard to accept that we are all one. Trauma and hardship make it difficult because we may view the external source of our trauma as evil or bad. It can be spiritually and emotionally challenging to accept that, in a way, we are them and they us. We are all one being.

Whether you view other lives literally as sequential life experiences or more generally as manifestations of our interconnection and oneness as humans, the truth is the same. We are one.

Do you feel this oneness and interconnection? If yes, you are ready to begin the process of consciously balancing your karma.

Spiritually balancing your karma is a journey. It is advanced only in the sense that it requires a deep sense of faith in spirit or the divine. You can fake this faith till you make it. It's even better if you truly feel it.

To begin, get comfortable and make sure you have fifteen or more minutes to work on this.

1. Say aloud, "I connect with my Higher Self. I ask that all that transpires during and associated with this process be for the highest good of all life and in accordance with universal Natural Law."
2. Breathe deeply and allow yourself to feel relaxed and at peace. Visualize an infinitely faceted jeweled sphere before you. What color do you picture this beautiful jeweled orb of light?

3. Notice the sphere before you revolving. It may be changing colors while doing this. This sphere holds the infinite totality of your relationship karma.
4. Reach your hands out to touch the sides of the sphere, almost like you are holding it, even though it is floating of its own accord.
5. Feel the sphere spin in your hands. Gaze into it with your inner vision, as if you are staring off into space. It may be very active in there or calm.
6. Say aloud, "I allow my relationship karma to be balanced. I ask that this process be pleasant. I trust that the Great Spirit/Divinity/Goddess/God and all of my spirit helpers will care for me with utmost tenderness throughout this experience and honor my focus and intention on joy, light, happiness, agreeable learning, and balanced ease. I ask to only balance and integrate as much karmic energy as I am prepared to digest easily and gently. I ask that my life only be enhanced by this process and my well-being grow as a result of it."
7. Simply notice any changes in the way the jeweled sphere looks, feels, and moves, and any feelings or sensory input you experience. Wait a couple of minutes to let the changes settle down.
8. Bring your hands back to your lap. State, "I release my relationship karma to the divine, that it might be transformed for the highest good." Watch the jeweled sphere dissolve.
9. Give yourself a few more minutes and then begin to bring your awareness back into the room. Notice your surroundings, feel whatever you are sitting in or lying on beneath you. Let go of the process with love and knowledge that you are enhanced.

Make sure you drink plenty of water and get a bit of extra sleep for a few days after this process. Keep your eyes open for any results of today's focused intention in your external life.

INSTEAD OF SETTLING FOR MEDIOCRE: DO THIS

Clear up your relationship karma as much as is comfortable and be patient for someone exemplary to come into your life. Skip mediocre relationships with questionable men. Don't be dazzled by your hormones and his pheromones; let them be a part of a greater whole. This greater whole is "the whole package."

Take the time to use your intuition and gut-knowing to discern who is right for you. Use all of your new self-knowledge and choose yourself. Love yourself deeply and be satisfied with the amazing life you create. Be patient and skip mediocrity in favor of the extraordinary. It is worth it. (And so are you!)

ENERGETIC PREDATORS IN THE DATING WORLD

What constitutes a spiritual man? He goes to metaphysical events? He talks the new-age talk? He wears eco-conscious clothing or crystal jewelry? Maybe. What you are really looking for in a dating partner is someone who is spiritual, yes, but also heart centered and energetically clear, clean, and in integrity.

Otherwise, you may find yourself dealing with an energetic predator. Energetic predators are relatively few. You certainly do not want to date these people! It is always good to be prepared and, in doing so, not be fearful of surprise situations. These predators can be found in all kinds of places: at metaphysical or spiritual events, commonly at bars or places where people are drinking heavily, at everyday places like the grocery store or other spots. They may be strangers or people you know. The attempt to invade your energy field can be random or caused by events. That is what an energetic predator does, tries to invade your energy field and often suck some energy off the top. Some events that inspire energetic invasion might be romantic rejection or something you have done to offend. It can also happen that you did or said nothing and they may simply be attracted to your light.

The key regarding energetic predators is to let go of your fear. Like sharks, they are attracted to fear. At this point on the planet we live in duality. There is light and dark, evolution and the opposite of evolution. One of the main challenges to master as a human being is to choose and attract the light. The more we are able to let go of our fear (the dark) the more light we attract. The exercises later in the chapter are about protection and awareness and they will help you eliminate some of your fears.

REPLACING FEAR WITH LOVE

The opposite of fear is love. You can tune in to your fears and allow them to gently be replaced with love.

1. Let yourself get into a relaxed and meditative state.

- Breathe deeply and move your awareness in to your heart. Ask that all that transpires in this exercise be for the highest good of all life and in accordance with universal Natural Law.
- State aloud, "I feel the deep love I have for myself. From this place of loving strength I choose to release any fears that no longer serve me at this time."
- Let your body tell you where the first fear energy is located. You will feel it as a knowing or a sensation.
- Go into the area with your awareness. Witness it. Feel the fear if you can, knowing you are in a safe place. Just allow it to be.
- If it is a fear that you can talk yourself through, do this. Tell yourself why you don't need to be afraid that your family members are going to die in a car accident every time they

drive. Only take a minute for this part. The body is where you want to keep most of your awareness.

- Now state, "I would like to completely replace this fear with divine love. This occurs immediately. It is done."
- Place your attention on the area where the fear was. How does it feel? Can you feel the divine love pumping into it? Notice.
- Go back through these steps for other fears or areas of the body that come up. You may not always be able to identify the fear; you may just feel it in your body. Say, "I will now allow the next fear to come forward in a place of love and acceptance." And repeat the pertinent steps above.

2. Lastly, when you feel like you have had enough for the moment, state, "I am love and all that is real is love. All else gently falls away. I allow this with and without my conscious participation. It is done."

If you have a serious fear, then you may want to seek out a clear and aligned healer who specializes in energy clearing and psychic protection and learn from him until you feel empowered and prepared.

Shine your light. Do not be afraid. You are a hot ticket and people are going to admire you and be attracted by your light and charisma, by your particular individual gifts. You need not fear energetic predators. You are powerful and strong and the light in you will always prevail. You will be aware and see your potential dates for who they are. Trust yourself and read on.

Being aware of energy exchanges will help you discern who is behaving in energetic integrity and who is not. As a longtime workshop facilitator at myriad conferences and expos, I can share some guidelines to keep your energy field and body at its clearest and healthiest level.

AWARENESS

Awareness of the energy that surrounds you will help you identify negative energetic fields and energetic predators—and do something about them.

1. Trust your instincts. The first part of awareness is trusting your instincts. When you feel that something is off with someone, it probably is. In these situations, examine any fears that might be influencing you. For example, I had an authority figure growing up who communicated the message that because you are a woman, you must be on constant lookout for male rapists, because they are everywhere. So, for me, it is important to take a moment to check if that is influencing my intuition about a person or situation. The more you work through fear issues from the past, the less they will influence your intuition.

2. Don't second-guess yourself. Trust your instincts and act. For example, if someone makes you uncomfortable, and you know it isn't simply a matter of them triggering a fear in you, then follow your instincts and leave the room or do whatever you feel compelled to do. Don't talk yourself out of listening to your instincts. Trust yourself. Sometimes energetic predators show up in non-physical form. They may be a nonphysical aspect of a real person you have met or an energy you cannot identify. It matters not what they are. If you sense an unfamiliar and unhelpful energy in the room, tell it to go. You can point your finger at it and hiss, then say, "Go!" Be forceful, strong and confident. Show no fear, for you are safe.

Claim your space. You own your space. State it: "I own my space. I own my life." Fully and totally inhabit your personal space. This is the sphere of energy surrounding you about three to five feet out all around you. It is big and you can fill it with light. State aloud, "I own my space! My life and being are totally filled with love-light and all else falls away. *Now*! It is done!" Claiming your space is about communication. You are setting and maintaining your boundaries clearly and with ease and strength.

PREVENTION

Use these tactics prior to entering a crowded situation or when you are feeling vulnerable or tired, or are simply feeling compelled that they are a good idea. You can use them each morning to keep yourself clear for the day.

Seal Yourself Up

State aloud, "I seal and protect all wormholes, portals, doorways, and openings in my physical and etheric bodies and in my auric egg, in all dimensions, all interdimensions, and all realities. I do this as needed for my highest good and the highest good of all life for all time." (Thank you to my teacher Laurie Levity Laughing Star for helping to develop this saying and for sharing the golden bodysuit concept described in this section.)

GOLDEN BODYSUIT

- Envision yourself putting on a bodysuit made of gold light. This bodysuit will cover each part of you in a continuous layer of protection.
- It stretches over your feet and between each toe. Feel it.
- It continues up over your ankles, calves, shins, knees.

- Pull it up over your thighs and pelvis. It covers all bodily openings and slightly indents into them with a gold layer of protective light fabric.
- Next, pull the golden suit up over your hips and stomach, fully covering your belly button.
- Now allow it to move up over your whole torso and chest, under and around your breasts, protecting them and allowing them to feel energetically safe.
- Now allow it to stretch down your arms, over each finger and your hands and covering your underarms.
- Grow the golden suit up over your shoulders, collarbone, throat, and neck.
- Then grow it up over your hair. It covers each hair and indents into each follicle with golden perfection. Your crown chakra on the top of your head is gently and completely shielded.
- Now pull it down over your face. It covers your eyelids and eyelashes (including follicles), growing under your eyelids with gentle protection. Then pull it over and around each eyeball.
- Continue growing your gold-light suit down over your face and nose, allowing it to gently indent into your nostrils.
- Next pull it down to coat your lips and mouth, growing inside and sheathing the inside of your mouth, tongue, and each individual tooth, with an ending curved pocket in the back of your throat, so the suit completely seals your mouth's inner and outer surface to the outside.
- Lastly, pull it down over your ears and their openings and your jaw, allowing it to connect to the rest of the suit so you are completely encased in golden-light protection.
- You can also sheathe your aura or auric egg that surrounds you in the same golden-light fabric suit. This will be an easy-to-pull-on sphere.

CLEARING

You can clear yourself from any unwanted energies using different techniques. Here are some of my favorites. They are all effective and can be used singly or in succession. Remember, you are powerful and you can reclaim your space. The stronger and more confident you become in your light-love power, the less you will feel invaded. Remember to claim your space. You are in charge of your reality. Claim it! Create it as you choose, with light and love.

- Disconnect for all time from the person or people who have invaded your personal or energetic space and those energies. Do this by stating the following aloud with intention: "I now disconnect from _____ (say the person's name if you know it, or say 'anyone who has invaded my psychic, energetic, or personal space in any way') for all time in all dimensions, all interdimensions, and all realities as needed for my highest good and the highest good of all life. I clear from my field all energies associated with this person/these persons and/or any associated situations from my life, affairs, being, and body for all time. In the spirit of gratitude, I ask that they be released from my focus for all time. It is done."
- In Chapter 7 we talked about soaking in a sea salt bath and smudging yourself to clear your energy field. Refer to those pages to do those exercises.
- You can also use the Violet Flame Energy Cleanse detailed in Chapter 2 to clear your auric field.

The techniques shared earlier in this chapter for prevention and clearing are tools to empower you to deal with anything energetic that comes your way. In that state of empowerment, you will attract more light. And if anything untoward happens, you are prepared.

Therefore, you can let go of your fear and know that if something occurs you can handle it.

As spiritual, and often psychically sensitive, women, we are best served in our dating life by being prepared. Having tools at our disposal to deal with any energetic predators, whether they are dates or just people we meet, can enhance our confidence in ourselves to handle situations and maintain our health and happiness.

Now, with all of that heavier stuff out of the way, we can move forward and talk about all of the yummy, delicious sensuality we may encounter when we are spiritually dating. Get ready to jump into the sea of love and lust! It can rock our worlds or lull us to sleep peacefully as we float along on a wave of lust chemicals.

Part Five

Deepen Your Intimacy

You have the opportunity to explore facets of your sexuality whether you're dating or not, but to be a conscious dater, you will fare better if you understand what is going on with your sex drive, how lust works, and what sacred sexuality means.

As biological beings, we have a cacophony of sexy sights, smells, and chemical triggers at play within and around us all of the time. And as spiritual daters whose intuitive senses are opening, we also have extrasensory, mystical abilities available for us to learn to use in our dating lives.

In the chapters in Part 5, we will discuss sacred sexuality. What is it? How does it apply to our lives as spiritual daters? How can we ascend into a new sexual and sensual paradigm, the highest and most satisfying expression of our sensual nature? It is not about who is the most spiritual in the sense of the ascetic and devout. It is about being present to your inner sensual nature and honoring it, listening to it and all of its innate body wisdom and inherent sacredness.

In this part of the guide, we remember how beautiful our love lives are meant to be.

Chapter Nine

The Aromatic Symphony

All around us, every day, a symphony of complex, organic beauty surrounds us. Wafts and breezes bring almost undetectable smells to us. We respond without thought, in accordance with our bodies' design. Our animal bodies respond to the chemical triggers released into the air by our peers. A world of aromas and their intertwining energies is like a web around us all. The aromatic symphony shapes our lives and behavior.

It therefore governs our dates in a major way. It tells us whether to be attracted or repelled by someone and them by us. The chemical zing we get from a guy's closeness and masculine smell needs to be there for us to feel deeply attracted. Some people will tell you it doesn't matter; it does. But it isn't the only factor. Many a woman has gotten into a relationship with the wrong guy because of a preference for his pheromones, the chemicals his body releases.

We must strike a balance between attraction's heady aphrodisiac qualities and emotionally based feelings of safety and general compatibility. Hold out for that balance.

Take in the information in the following sections to bring awareness to how you have dated in the past. Has it been pheromone based? Cast an eye to the future, toward a balanced awareness of the power of the chemicals of attraction. Then when you feel the attraction of the aromatic symphony, you can make informed decisions that take into account all of the factors influencing you.

PHEROMONES AND THE CHEMICALS OF ATTRACTION

You know the feeling that overtakes you when someone smells so good you just want to pounce? Or when you are inexplicably attracted to someone you don't even know? Welcome to the world of the chemicals of attraction! They are powerful forces in our lives. In this chapter, we will learn to use them to enhance our dating lives, not to rule them.

First, we need to understand what is going on inside of and around our bodies. Pheromones are *smell signals* intended to compel us to act. As researchers Karl Grammer, Bernhard Fink, and Nick Neave have shown in their studies, pheromones tell us a lot about our genetic compatibility with a potential sexual partner. Perhaps they evolved to create the strongest babies most likely to survive in a sometimes harsh world. Now, they entice us and create behaviors born of instinct. Mmmm, delicious. And, yet, dangerous.

Have you felt the rush of pheromone-borne attraction? If you have ever felt passionately attracted to someone, then the answer is yes. It starts the fire burning. Let's examine whether that has been productive in our lives. Most of us have felt a powerful pheromone rush, an undeniable attraction. At its best, it is mixed with an instant psychic understanding of the other's good, authentic essence.

On the other hand, rushes of pheromone attraction have also led us down some relationship roads that were better left untrod. Pheromones can sometimes make a meeting feel as if a great love story has begun. In some cases, it is simply chemical! Have you had any experiences that, looking back, you would attribute to the effects of pheromones? Were they positive or ultimately not?

KISSING AND LICKING

Don't you love a good kiss? When it is right, it never gets old. A kiss bonds us and inspires feelings of closeness and intimacy. Over 90 percent of people on planet Earth kiss each other!

A nice bit of licking is intimate and primal. Why do people do it? What inspires us to transfer our saliva back and forth as a romantic gesture? Testosterone!

The male sex chemical testosterone stimulates sex drive. "There is evidence that saliva has testosterone in it," says Rutgers University anthropologist Helen Fisher. "And there is evidence that men like sloppier kisses with more open mouth. That suggests they are unconsciously trying to transfer testosterone to stimulate sex drive in women."

After a great kissing session have you ever felt more interested in a man than prior? That might be the saliva talking! Awareness is the key. Understanding our bodies' chemical drives and motivations helps us notice how our behavior is affected.

When we date, the urge to kiss means that the chemicals of attraction are working. Notice the additional factors, too. What inspires you to want to kiss someone? An endearing story he told where he let himself be a little vulnerable? Does that sensitivity turn you on? Or are you kissing to comfort someone you are bonding with?

On dates, a kiss can tell us a lot. Does it feel good to be close to the date? Does it have that rightness that is a combination of chemical compatibility, energetic compatibility, feelings of emotional safety, and a clicking of personalities? How does he handle the kiss? Is he masculine, taking charge of it . . . or gentle and sweet . . . or a heady combination of both?

What do you like in a kiss? What does it tell you about the date? Lots of women will tell you that they are not sure about someone until they kiss him. They need to feel that sensual connection to assess whether they want to be friends or dates. It is important.

Keep in mind the mixing of energies. Wait to kiss till it is the right time. Keep your energy field clear by being discerning about whom you kiss and when. No one was ever worse off for delaying a kiss in favor of getting to know someone a bit more first.

Even your lips are sacred. The people who touch them must know you are sacred and know this about themselves, too. Practice sacred kissing. It is more casual than sex, but it is still special. Sacred kissing happens between two people who have recognized their own and the other's sacredness. These people see even their lips as beautiful, sexy expressions of the divine. This type of kissing feels extra good. It feels not only loving but emotionally safe and pleasurable. Often it is even more of a turn-on than a conventional kiss. The energy exchanged between the two people is clear and high-vibe. Respect and love yourself and demonstrate this to yourself by being discerning about your kisses. Make them special!

ENDORPHINS . . . NOT JUST FOR RUNNERS ANYMORE

First, you are kissing. The testosterone is revving things up. Then, touching begins and . . . Pow! The starting gun is shot, just as if you are running a race. Endorphins flood your body. Runner's high becomes toucher's high.

Plenty of research has shown that touching releases endorphins. Some foreplay might substitute nicely for your morning run. Feel-good chemicals keep the action going. Again, awareness is key. Noticing ourselves in the present and examining past situations can help us consciously choose behaviors that are healthy for us.

When you begin dating someone seriously, eventually you will start fooling around. This gives you a preview of how your sexual relationship might be, which is important information that gets you ready to make decisions about whether to have sex with someone or not.

The same principles of sacredness apply to touching as to kissing, but even more so. When you engage in sexual activity with someone, your vital life force gets mixed with theirs. When it is right, this is a natural, positive energy exchange. However, either you have to know someone pretty well to know that their field is healthy and that you want to bond in this way or your intuition has to be very sure and strong that it is healthy and enhancing to your well-being to fool around with this person.

Be aware that endorphins make us want more endorphins, which translates into wanting more intimate touching and sex. They are part of nature's ploy to get us to propagate the species. These chemicals can become a resource for pleasure, but they need to be managed with awareness.

Remember, you are sacred and people you are with should view you, and themselves, as such. This is all about the heart. Love, not chemicals, should fuel your impetus to kiss and touch. Your heart center, a very special and beautiful part of your energy body in the center of your chest, happens to be located in an area that gets frequently involved in foreplay. Prizing your sacredness and remembering that behind your beautiful breasts is your loving heart will help you make sure that only those who are kind and see you and themselves as sacred get close to you there.

OXYTOCIN: THE BONDING CHEMICAL

Another feel-good chemical, oxytocin, is released during orgasm (and also during breast-feeding!). Research tells us that oxytocin makes us bond and feel a sense of well-being. Oxytocin is nature's way of telling us to stay with the person who triggers it, whether they are a lover or baby. Women are especially prone to this bonding. We are motivated to have sex to connect, whether for a night or a lifetime. Couple that predisposition to crave connection with a powerful hit of oxytocin after sex and, as women, we are bonding significantly.

Sometimes it's simply the chemical factor that influences us to stay with a romantic partner for a longer time than is best for us. The chemicals make us feel bonded. The same factors make a one-night stand look like a potential life partner; the love chemicals are telling us to stay. So we do, sometimes, and we have sex again and the oxytocin keeps strengthening the urge to stay bonded.

You can see how the oxytocin released during orgasm could make a partner who is not well-suited to us look better than his reality. This is a situation where reality sometimes gets obscured. Has this ever happened to you?

An example: Penny had been single for a few years and she was feeling lonely and sexually frustrated (a good vibrator might have prevented the forthcoming mess). She was on vacation with friends, most of whom were married, when she met Jesse. They were out at a bar and not necessarily thinking clearly. Penny and Jesse ended up in a drunken hookup. The next morning she left, not feeling good for lots of reasons. In her hungover state, she began to think of Jesse as a potential partner. Might that work? She had heard whisperings the night before that he might be engaged. Her friends could see he was shady, at best.

Later that day it was confirmed: Jesse was engaged to a woman back in San Francisco. That night Penny saw him out again and the hookup was repeated. This continued for much of the vacation. And she still considered a potential future with this guy! She knew she wasn't doing anything positive for herself but still she continued the self-destructive behavior. Why?

How much of a role did the oxytocin released during orgasm play? Did it bond Penny to Jesse in repeated chemical doses? What about the other chemicals we discussed? Testosterone from saliva, endorphins from touching—did they knock Penny's good sense out of her temporarily?

They played a role in influencing a typically healthy woman who was feeling emotionally vulnerable to abuse herself. The chemicals alone cannot do this—the preexisting emotional and psychological states need to be there, too—but nature's potentially beautiful chemical helpers can become a bad influence.

At our best, when we are feeling emotionally healthy, self-actualized, and centered, the chemicals of attraction can enhance a positive, affirming relationship by allowing both people to bond and appreciate pleasure together through lovemaking. That is the highest expression of the chemicals of attraction. When experienced with awareness, these chemicals can be a radiant and ecstatic enhancement to a conscious, loving dating life.

KNOWLEDGE TURNS THE CHEMICALS OF ATTRACTION INTO OUR ALLIES

Now that you have an idea of the way some chemicals in your body try to get you to mate, you can modulate those urges with good sense and a deep sense of self-love and respect. When you are an aware, conscious woman, you date with authority. You own your life and your space. You are empowered and allow the chemicals of attraction to be your allies. This happens because you are aware of how they affect you. Can you think of cases where the chemicals of attraction got you involved with someone you would not have otherwise chosen? Can you count on yourself to be more aware next time? To be even more on top of your well-being and make choices that are respectful of your sacredness? If yes, then you're ready for the following exercise.

HARMONIZE YOUR HEART, MIND, AND BODY CHEMISTRY

Give your body the message that you are going to keep it safe, happy, healthy. The body on its own needs help to best manage itself.

- Make a commitment to listen to your body. Take some time to really ask it what it needs and wants. Listen.
- Tell your body that you are committed to caring for it in the best way possible. That you will keep it safe and healthy and your body can trust you to do this. Do this out loud. Your body hears what you say. Talk to it to program it!
- Feel any resistance or unease in your body. Breathe into it and bring your awareness into that area and again honor your commitment to listen.

When you have committed to listen to your body, you are more able to deal with lust chemicals in the moment and follow through on the guidelines that you develop for yourself in the next section.

CREATING YOUR PERSONAL GUIDELINES FOR SEXUAL BEHAVIOR

Emotional maturity is an essential ingredient in a healthy, sacred sex life. One way to prevent the surge of chemicals in the moment from overriding your good sense is to create a set of guidelines to help you govern your dating life in relation to your sexuality. You can create this list and personalize it. Think of the list when you are tempted to engage in any type of physical connection with another person. Here is a list of suggestions to get you started:

- Only engage in sexual activity with people who see you and themselves as sacred beings.
- Take it slowly. You have plenty of time.
- Kiss when you feel close enough to the person to share some of your feelings uncensored.
- Engage in making out only after you have gotten to know each other for awhile. Wait until you feel comfortable talking about your relationship and what you are each looking for in your dating experience. Do your desires match?
- Get into more serious, unclothed sexual activity only when you feel 100 percent comfortable. You are sharing a sacred part of yourself and you must feel completely loved and accepted. Anything else can inspire trauma.
- Only have sex with someone when love and sacredness are flowing freely and are openly acknowledged by both of you. Give serious consideration to how you will feel after the sex. You should already know where the relationship is going and feel excellent about it. You should be able to discuss almost anything, including your and his emotional and relationship issues, sexual health and diseases or concerns, and sexual histories.

SMELLING YOUR DATES: ETHERIC PHEROMONES

Have you ever smelled someone before you saw them? This etheric, or intuitive, sense can happen even if you're not in the physical presence of another person. It happened to Jeanne. She describes it as intuitive and transcendent: "My friend Kate had been trying to set me up with this guy friend of hers, Micah, for months. I was off men after a painful breakup. At that time, I just needed a break.

"About a month later, my computer had an unfixable virus problem. The people at the local chain electronics store said to get another computer. But it was less than a year old. Kate suggested Micah look at it. He is a computer genius. We set up a time to meet at his office. As the day neared, I began to smell the most delicious chemical type of smell. I would dream about it. That day I felt like I was getting ready for a date with giddy sense of anticipation. Of course, my rational mind argued that I was being silly. As I drove to Micah's office, I smelled it again. It triggered all of the chemicals of attraction in my body before even meeting him, or that is how it felt, anyway.

"I arrived and instantly knew Micah from the rest of the group working around the communal-style office. We were both a little speechless at first. The energy buzzing between us was intense. In fact, it was intoxicating. We sat down in the common area at a table and booted up the computer, and right away with no thought about it, we sat close. Our legs touched under the table the whole time. And the mystery love-smell, it was there, coming from Micah.

"He did fix the computer in spite of the massive distraction of this overwhelming, loving impulse to just start going at it right on the table. We found more reasons to see each other. I would smell the Micah-smell, and a few minutes later he would call me. I would dream elaborate sexual love-fantasies of him and smell him. Then he would tell me the next day over the phone that he had a dream about me the night before, and in the beginning not mention any details. Weeks later when I asked him, he admitted the dreams were sensual. We finally got together, and of course you know the rest, 'cause you were at our wedding," she concluded with a smile.

"Does the chemical smell remain, even years later?" I asked curiously.

"Definitely," Jeanne answered. "It's not there all of the time. But when we feel sexy or are thinking of each other, it wafts into my psychic space."

When you are dating, it can be useful to be able to sense these etheric smells. They can inform you about the person you are dating and about your compatibility together. Wouldn't it be nice to be able to smell things about people's character, personality, and your chemical and intimate mixing together?

Like all of our potential intuitive senses, we can develop an olfactory psychic sense. Anyone can do this! We all have intuition, anyway; it is simply a matter of opening up this particular avenue. You can use it to enhance your dating life and smell your dates! Instinctual and intuitive information is readily available to enhance your dating life.

Everyone has intuitive abilities waiting to be tapped into. Lots of people can open their olfactory intuitive senses on their own. For some people it is innate. Yours may already be open and in effect. If they aren't, it is easy to activate them.

OPEN YOUR PSYCHIC SMELL SENSES

You can open up your psychic smell senses, including your ability to smell etheric pheromones. Simply follow the process below.

- State aloud, "I ask that all that transpires during this meditation be for the highest good of all life and in accordance with universal Natural Law, helping all and harming none."
- Next, state aloud, "I *am* my Higher Self. I allow my Higher Self to merge with my being in perfect harmony. I connect with my spirit family and the archangelic realm for guidance and loving support."
- Say aloud, "I ask that I be protected fully during this process and enveloped in pure love."
- Breathe deeply and quiet your body and mind.

- State aloud, "I now allow my psychic sense of smell to gently open. I let this sense only enhance my existence. I trust divine presence to provide me with ease in all ways. My senses are all self-correcting and self-regulating and they all function for my optimum and highest good. It is done."
- Place your hands on your heart center and rest quietly in the enveloping sense of pure love for at least seven minutes before continuing your day.

Now that you have opened your psychic smell senses, you will be able to learn to use this skill to improve your dating life. Notice your gut instincts about people. Your new super-smell senses will give you information in an instinctive way. You will just know if someone in your office is crushing on you. The smell will tell you either literally (you actually smell the scent of their attraction) or intuitively (you just know he likes you in a instinctive way).

The more present to the moment you are, the better the new smell senses will work. The more mindful you are of the way your body feels generally and when moving through space, the better your intuitive senses will work.

So, with all this new knowledge you can make more informed decisions. In the office crush example, you would either flirt with him if you were interested in him too or be extremely professional so as not to encourage his feelings if you didn't return them. Your new senses give you more choices of how to behave because you have more information. You can be even more on top of your dating life this way. You can sniff out a potential date and, as you learn to trust your instincts, gauge your compatibility. How handy! Be present with your sacred self and listen to your intuition.

Chapter Ten
Sacred Sex

Sacred sex is deeply loving sex with a spiritual bent between two people who see each other and themselves as sacred. Two people looking deeply into each other's eyes, murmuring words of love, encouragement, and praise to each other, expressing their profound, heartfelt love for each other may be practicing sacred sex. Sacred sex sometimes feels like your two bodies are fusing together as one, as if you are one being. We are all one, and sacred sex taps into that deep connection between two people. With a mind to the possibility of sacred sex, you can select dating partners who are capable of deep levels of the alchemical miracle that is love.

The right sacred-sex partner can support you and you can support him in ways that you both may have never felt. In that right union, you can know real safety and deep emotional comfort.

Hold the intention of attracting that caliber of man. He is emotionally mature, always growing, knows that you and he are sacred, loves and supports you with all his heart and being, holds space for you to heal any wounded parts of your sexuality, and lets you do the same for him.

That is the kind of man you can have sacred sex with. Sacred sex between two emotionally mature people who see each other as sacred expressions of the divine feminine and masculine can be as wild and racy as both people would like, but there is always a deep undercurrent of sacred love. It is beautiful. Hold out for it. It is how sex is meant to be for spiritual, conscious people.

THE HEART

The heart is more than a physical organ. It is the seat of our love, of our *heartfelt* emotion. It is a space where love from the universe flows into us—and back out. Our hearts are a sacred and special part of our being; they deserve to be honored and revered. Hold out for the person who can go to deep heartfelt depths of love with you. Wait for the man who sees you as sacred and whom you see as sacred, too. Then sexual love will grow, blossom, and radiate through everything; it is radiant beauty.

CONNECTING WITH HEART POWER

For women, it is important to notice that the heart is located in an area of your body that often gets lots of sexual attention. Many people regard that part of the female body, the breasts, as sex objects. Therefore, we need to love them extra! Our breasts are part of our heart. They are a sacred, sexual portal right into our hearts. They connect our sexuality with our hearts. Remember that you can own your space and not allow yourself to feel objectified. You can love and empower the sacredness of your breasts.

Our breasts have enormous energetic potential, and it has nothing to do with their size. Our breasts carry the energy of the nurturing aspects of the heart. They are our body's caretaker energy centers. Their power vibrates through us and it is a seemingly gentle, caring, loving energy that, in truth, is hugely powerful and sacred. We can embrace this part of ourselves as super sacred and honor it as part of our radiant female heart.

So, if a man is going to touch your breasts, he needs to see them as sacred. He needs to feel and understand that you are a representation of the divine feminine and that is why you have a beautiful female body. Settle for nothing less. Remember that you are sacred.

You Are the Divine Feminine

The divine feminine is the womb or void and receptivity. It is the yin in the yin-and-yang symbol. It is the receptive open beauty of the divine that receives the active light of the divine. The divine feminine is the ecstatic, nurturing, powerful, gentle, beautiful, creating, and destroying, full embodiment of the full power of the feminine principle of divinity. You are the divine feminine. You have a radiant female body made to experience the divine feminine through you and as you. You can experience yourself as sacred by reveling in the part of you that is the divine feminine. You embody it. You are it. Live it. Sacred sex is about you, embodying the divine feminine, merging with your guy, embodying the divine masculine. We will talk a bit more about the divine masculine later in the chapter.

MALE LIFE ENERGY

For men, the process is similar: Their hearts are loving, full, and beautiful when open. Obviously that is what you want in a partner—an open-hearted, loving man. However, although they do have breasts, men do not experience as much sensual or sexual connection to their hearts through their breasts. In men, the testicles function similarly to the female breast. To understand their energetic potential, think of them as Chinese stress balls. You know the ones you spin around each other in your hand and they have bells or some kind of resonant way of making sound in them? They vibrate.

That is what testicles do. They vibrate with the held energy of life and abundance. It is within them. They hold a heart-like energy when in their highest expression. They have the potential to hold the power of infinite love in action. When you are sexual with a man, treat his testicles as sacred, just as he should with your breasts. Sacred sexuality is an expression of each of you seeing each other and yourselves as sacred, sexual beings and making love from that place.

THE HARA (THE CENTER)

The "hara" is the Taoist term for the "seat of energy" located in your abdomen. For women, this includes the female reproductive area. It is where your power flows from. Have you ever noticed that your power is sensual and feminine? This is why! Your hara, inherently sacred and sensual, is a powerhouse—and it is you. You can hold and sustain a living human being in your hara! It is amazing whether or not you ever choose to do it.

Your hara is sacred. Many men will want to receive some of its goodness through sexual activity. Remember, though, that it is for you, not the masses. When you find your sacred soul mate, you and he will be able to have an equal exchange of hara energy and love. With an honest, sacred man, you can share your powerful female hara energy with his equally powerful male hara energy.

HARA POWER = GIRL POWER!
Tap into your seat of energy to empower yourself and tap into the powerful energy source of creativity inside of you. You will be

more creative, more powerful, more female in your beauty and you can heal yourself with your hara power.

- Lie down on your back or side or sit comfortably.
- Breathe deeply and relax.
- Place your hands on your hara, the low center of your abdomen, cupping it and holding it lovingly.
- Breathe with it and begin to tune in to it.
- Feel the power of your hara beneath your hands. Let it get stronger.
- Affirm internally that it is safe for you to be powerful. Tell your hara it is time to let your full power flow through you.
- Stay present and feel this power radiating through you.
- It may not flow out of you. It is self-regulating and will go where it needs to for your highest good.
- Affirm this now. Say aloud, "I allow my hara power to amplify and fully express itself. I allow this power to be self-regulating for the highest good and to only enhance my reality. So be it."
- The power of your hara can heal you and itself. If your hara feels wounded or scarred from trauma, whether from surgery there or sexual abuse or something else, your own hara power can heal you. It is an enormously powerful force within you. To access your hara's innate healing power, say the following: "I now allow my hara to unleash its massive healing power on my entire body and being. I ask that this healing be for my very highest good and in accordance with universal Natural Law, which means helping all and harming none. I let go of all energies that are not mine and/or are not for my best and let the area where they were be filled with the universal life power of my hara. Wounds now heal. Trauma is now released.

I allow my hara to feel new, fresh, clear, and full of love. My sexual center is free and clear and loved. I am love."

- Sit with this sensation in your body for as long as you feel compelled. Really feel it and revel in what a gift it is. Be grateful for your beautiful female body!

MEN'S HARA

Men have a hara energy of a different nature. It is equally sacred when loved and cultivated by a spiritual man. The man has a wand of light with alchemical potential woven through it energetically. Their wand and entire hara area are infused with the principle of the divine masculine: light and action. It is the yang in the yin and yang. The male actively gives through penetration and the female receives his wand of light. The female is receptive creation and the male is active creation in the world. The man's hara is the place where active creation energy enters the man's body and then quickly pops up the head to become the active principle.

THE GALAXY MEETS THE WIZARD'S WAND

Imagine your beautiful female sexual energy. It orbits throughout your uterus and reproductive organs. At its center, in the center of your uterus, is a portal, a magical place that transcends time and space. When a woman is pregnant, it is the place where souls come through to be incarnated, but it is much more than that.

It is a portal from which you can bring anything you desire into this dimension. It is a galaxy with a gateway at its center. When you bring a wand of light—a loving partner's penis—into the center of this galaxy, alchemy happens.

The galaxy is lit to life with the power of the wand of light. The wand can enliven and activate the energy of potential within the uterus and create something real in your life! It is magic but is not mystical and unattainable. You can do it. I am not just talking about creating a baby. I am talking about creating anything you want in life: a new career, a different home, a happier family. And it doesn't matter if the woman is unable to have a baby or has been through menopause. The galaxy is forever creative as is the female spirit.

All the power and beauty of the universe is within you and a wand of light from your true love will let it come forth in the best, most perfect way possible. Wait for your true love and live the magic of sacred sexuality.

SEX IS CONNECTION

Sex is all about connection. You connect with yourself and your loved one in the deep transcendence of sacred sex. You open yourself to receive your man and he puts himself forward and immerses himself within you. It is a joining of two beings.

You are naturally psychic and empathetic (we all are) and when you connect so closely with someone, you can know him even more deeply. And you let yourself be known—no walls, no barriers, just truth. That is what sacred sex is all about: truth.

It takes courage to let your truth be seen. That is why you must make sure that you are seeing the sacred in your partner and that he is seeing the sacred in you. In that safety, you can truly connect.

Your connection might be fun and silly one day while your lovemaking echoes with laughter and merriment. Another day, it might be wild and primal while you bite and scratch and unleash your animal selves. On a different (or the same) night, your lovemaking might be deep and sensual where you sink deeply into each other in profound love. Yet another time, it might be tender and sweet when the two of you heal your hearts and bare your souls.

Whatever guise the sacred sex wears, it is a connection through which you share yourself with someone wonderful and beautiful. You revel in and honor each other's truth.

TYPES OF SACRED SEX

Sacred sex is imbued with the love of the divine and the love of the two people involved. As we discussed in Chapter 7, Sacred Lovemaking is sex with real respect and love for each other plus a deep spiritual connection, most often experienced between partners who are monogamous and committed to each other. It is heart centered and deeply honoring.

With sacred sex, it is a given that you respect and honor each other and have a high-functioning, emotionally healthy relationship. When you are dating, you can begin to gauge if your dates, as you get to know them, might be capable of sacred sex with you when you are both ready and if circumstances are right. You can gauge this by noticing whether a date is spiritually open and adept. Does he understand the concept of sacredness (yours and his) and does he live it? As you get to know each other, get him to open up about his ideas of sacredness and see if he has any thoughts on sacred sexuality. If he has already given the topic a lot of thought and is aligned with it, that is a good sign.

Sacred Marriage Lovemaking is sacred sex with an extra dose of sacred. It is between people who are married or committed to each other for a lifelong bond. The lifelong bond creates an even deeper sense of safety and emotional security. Often, any residual sexual and emotional issues can be healed in the act of Sacred Marriage Lovemaking.

The spiritual connection between partners can be cultivated but not faked. It is authentic. You each have to be willing to bare yourselves and your souls to each other. This connection is fostered by clear, honest communication. Both partners must accept and love each other unconditionally, as themselves, totally, completely, nothing hidden; you meet in the arena of sensual pleasure and honor each other with ecstasy and love. And from there, as long as you honor each other as sacred beings and respect each other, anything goes. Does this sound idyllic or make you ask yourself, are any men capable of this? The answer is yes. There are men looking for depth in a relationship and they know how to see your sacredness and honor women. They are out there. And there only needs to be one, the right one, whom you are compatible with, for you. Solo sex is also sacred! It is a beautiful way to love yourself. We will talk about it more later in this chapter.

RECOGNIZING YOUR PARTNER AND BEING RECOGNIZED

Imagine a partner who loves and accepts you to a degree where you feel genuinely comfortable sharing your full self. You know that this person is not judging you, that his love for you is transcendent, that you can share your vulnerabilities, fears, hurts, thoughts, dreams, everything.

Now imagine being that present for someone else—loving your partner that much and trusting him so deeply that you can truly accept him for who he is. Feel how free and liberating that would be, to know that someone is so good and worthy of your love and trust, and that he feels the same way about you. This is recognizing your partner and being recognized. It is a gift of the experience of spiritual marriage or long-term partnership.

Varying degrees of this mutual recognition exist in relationships. The ultimate accepting and recognizing of each other signals a deep love and sacred knowing of each other's beauty. You are worthy of this! You are that beautiful, inside and out. Hold out for a partner who will see you in all of your beauty: your flaws and strengths and your full truth.

Set Your Sexual Sights High

Sacred Marriage Lovemaking occurs between married or life-partnered couples and is done with specific healing and uplifting intentions set by the couple. This type of sacred sex reaches even deeper levels of sensual and spiritual merging. People who are in a lifelong relationship and explore sacred sexuality report a deepening of their already existing bond and a sweet richness to the quality of their lovemaking. For many, it is an experience encountered only with their spiritual soul mate.

- Do you seek this level of union for yourself? It is attainable.
- If yes, set your intention now; state it aloud. "I will meet and partner with (or marry) my spiritual soul mate, my true love, and I choose for all sex to be sacred and ecstatic for the rest of my days."
- When dating you can remember that this is your goal, it is what you have set your intention upon, and settle for nothing less than it.

HEALING THROUGH SACRED SEX

Sacred sex is a potentially healing experience. A client we will call Sadie had boyfriends during the forty-five years of her life. She had varying relationships and some were positive and some were not. When she met Payton, they connected deeply on a spiritual level. They took their sexual relationship slowly, waiting for it to be right. When they finally made love, they were really ready.

Over the course of months, their spiritual bond continued to deepen. For each of them, some sexual issues came up. Sadie had felt used in some of her past sexual experiences. Payton could see that in her, and as those issues came up in her body, he looked in her eyes and repeated his love for her. He showed her he was present with her and only her. This was repeated and eventually these feelings and issues in Sadie dissolved. There was even more space than before for their divine, loving connection. They were happy and grateful. When Payton's issues arose months later about being rejected sexually by his ex, Sadie was there, being present and loving him through them. They both healed deeply through sacred sexuality.

MAKING SEX MORE SPIRITUAL

To make sex more spiritual you can:

- Light candles and set the mood.
- Spend time talking about all the things you love about each other and your relationship before having sex.
- Shower together and wash each other, expressing love and complimenting each other's inner and outer beauty.
- Discuss your sexual and body image issues as they arise. Listen to each other and make space for these things to come up even during sex, then be present to them together. Love each other and support each other during these instances.
- Reframe sex to be not only about orgasm but about bonding and merging your hearts and spirits.
- Scatter organic flower petals on the bed and sprinkle them over each other. This beauty symbolizes the beauty of your hearts, souls, bodies, spirits.
- Be intimate in and out of the bedroom. Be close and be best friends.
- Be sensual with each other in nature. Kiss outside on a hike. Fool around in the ocean. This connects you both with each other and with nature, exposing you to more divine and earthy or watery energy while feeling it course through your bodies. You are both part of nature. It is a sacred and primal part of your beings.

- Create things together. Do art together in the buff. Cook together and feed each other with your hands. Be creative and sensual together, sharing yourselves.
- Always, always, always without fail be respectful of each other and mindful of each other's sacredness. It will resonate through your union.

SOLO SACRED SEX

Sex with yourself can be just as sacred and just as powerful as sex with your soul mate. In fact, hopefully, even when you are with your soul mate you will still take time to love yourself, too.

Sacred sex means being filled with love and seeing the divine within all involved. If you are the only one involved, then you simply must see the sacred in yourself. In doing so, you give your cells the message that sex is now steeped in love and sacredness. Think how healing that has the potential to be!

You can create a new sexual and sensual groove or pattern for yourself by loving yourself in a sexual and sensual way while being fully aware of and honoring your sacredness. This new pattern will resonate through your future sex life. You can pre-pattern it with recognition of sacredness and deep self-love.

- To do this, set the stage with loving music, candles, soft lighting, whatever gets you in a love-filled and sensual mood. Maybe take a nice hot bath.
- Next, set an intention for your self-lovemaking. For example, seek ecstatic sacred pleasure and loving, easy healing for body, heart, mind, spirit, and soul.

- Make love to yourself in whatever way you feel like. Let yourself be uninhibited. Go with what feels good and love filled for you. Focus on your sacredness.
- Keep your intention in mind and repeat any simple affirmations in your mind or aloud if you feel the urge. Some good ones are: "I am sacred"; "I am love"; "I love myself"; "I am the sacred feminine"; "I am the goddess."
- Make your lovemaking an expression of your love for yourself. That is where sex comes from, a place of love.

ENERGETIC SEXUAL COMMUNION

Remember Jeanne from Chapter 9? She smelled her future husband before she ever met him. After her and Micah's first few dates, something kind of amazing started to happen. She would be doing something low-key such as napping or reading, and sensual thoughts of her and Micah would come forward in her consciousness. In the dream image or fantasy, they would be kissing and close together, and it felt very similar to when they were physically together—just less physical sensation and more spiritual energy flowing between them. In Jeanne's case, she also smelled him, even though he wasn't there.

Micah says that he never smelled Jeanne's smell but that he felt a similar energetic sexual communion at the same times that she did. The two of them were connected across space and time. Love transcends everything, including space and time, and their love and desire for each other created an energetic interaction. I do not recommend energetic sexual communion as a novel thing you try out with a guy you just kind of like. If you open those doors with someone you do not love and feel committed to long-term, you will very likely wish you hadn't. Because they can be harder to close than open.

ETHERIC SEX HAPPENS!

When a sexual connection is strong between two people, etheric sex can happen. It is energetic sex—that is, sex with our spirits. Most commonly it happens with intention and conscious knowledge of each other. In those cases, couples who are apart connect energetically and emotionally through the medium of love. Their love for each other flows and etheric lovemaking can occur. You can imagine it as the way angelic beings might make love. The human body can feel this in the usual physical ways or in more energetic ways, such as with pulsing energy and tingling sensations.

Rarely, etheric sex can occur between people who have yet to meet or have only met briefly. This is something that is under the jurisdiction of the two people's Higher Selves. And in these cases Natural Law is very important to remember: Helping All, Harming None. Etheric sex *must* be completely consensual—otherwise it is a psychic attack of a very damaging kind. Attempted forced etheric sex is like an energetic assault. However, something like this can only happen if you allow it on some level. If you clearly own your space, you fill your own auric field up and there are no openings or little holes for someone to try to get in, then no one can ever try to force any kind of energetic interaction on you whether you are aware of it or not. Remember, you own your space. You fill your being and the area surrounding you with your energy.

To affirm this you can state, "I own my space." When doing so, feel your energy fill your body and the area around in a sphere about five feet out in all directions. You can easily protect yourself from psychic attack. You are safe, by owning your space. Your ex, for example, can't force you to have etheric sex. The creepy guy you met also cannot hurt you etherically. You are strong and full of power. You own your space. We talked about owning your space and related topics in Chapter 8.

It is important that we are conscious about our actions as well. Fantasy with a "hologram" of someone we are attracted to is fine. In that case we are acknowledging that he is not really with us. We are just attracted to him or what he represents for us. Go ahead and think about George Clooney or whomever floats your boat. But just as you would not want someone to energetically attack you, you do not want to harm others. You must make certain your intention is clear and harmless.

A NEW SEXUAL PARADIGM

Sacredness is the new sexual revolution. It is a new paradigm, available for your conscious choosing. You may be in the minority now, or so it may seem. However, there are many spiritual people of all genders and orientations out there who are looking for something more, something honoring and sacred. These people will find each other. And their numbers will grow.

The new sexual paradigm of sacredness is a choice you can make. Being conscious will help you avoid those who are not ready for it. You will see who has sacredness-vision and share healthy intimacy when the time is right. Trust the new paradigm and yourself. Embrace it and let yourself be an inspiration to others with your behavior.

Part Six

Stay the Course
of Lovingkindness

Lovingkindness is a way of being that focuses on loving acceptance of yourself and others. With such a positive focus, you can't help but attract positive people and situations. Staying the course and committing to lovingkindness, especially toward yourself, will help you draw forth your spiritual soul mate. Because you dwell in the space and vibration of lovingkindness, your eventual mate will, too.

In this part of the book, we will define all of the soul mate vernacular. Twin flames, divine complements, soul mates: I'll give you my definitions based on more than ten years as a medical intuitive and conscious dating coach. You'll learn about the spiritual implications of your mate and his arrival in your life.

We will also talk about you. You are important! We'll talk about how to have faith in yourself and how to trust yourself with love. You deserve the best.

Chapter Eleven

Everything in the Universe Conspires to Bring Your Soul Mate

Everything in the universe is conspiring to bring you and your true love together. All of your unseen helpers—you might call them spirit guides—are rooting for you to meet your mate at the perfect time for both of you. The universe is served by you and your soul mate being together. Together you live more joyfully, and you radiate more happiness and harmony. When you are in joy, your vibe is higher. If your vibe is higher, the Earth and all existence benefit!

SOUL MATES, TWIN FLAMES, AND DIVINE COMPLEMENTS

The human heart craves partnership on many levels. This craving inspires stories of fairy-tale meetings and Cinderella dreams in our minds and the media. On some level these tales speak to our hearts. Yes, we are independent women. We do not *need* a man to validate us, but many of us long to share our lives with that certain someone we often call The One. Why? Why is there one? Is there *just* one?

Emotionally, you, like all humans, crave to show your true colors to a mate who loves and accepts you. Emotionally, your heart is wired to want The One. You are built to seek your spiritual soul mate. True love aligns you with your true self because you cannot find it if you are not your true, authentic self. You have to be real—the real thing—to find the real thing. It is the universe's way of getting you (and all of us) to be authentic!

You crave physical closeness. It's a basic human need to be touched. When your true love touches you, having that physical need met is even more satisfying. On a chemical level, touch seems even more powerful when given by someone you love, whether the touch is sexual or day-to-day affection and comfort. Once you have it, you don't want to settle for anything less.

Even mentally, you crave your partner. This is the person who understands you, who is mentally in tune with you. Spiritually, your true love fills a need in you to be seen as the divine being you are. Sometimes the way your partner sees you enlivens your view of yourself. It shows you how radiant you are as you simultaneously see your partner's own dazzling spiritual radiance. It is a beautiful spiritual circle of love.

Love is the magnetic factor that pulls you to your soul mate and the glue that keeps you there. Love's power is infinite. It heals anything. It is balm when you hurt and boosts your joy when you are happy. Love is made of spiritual and emotional energy commingled into something amazing. It is what you look for when you date. It is what you will find manyfold when you give it to yourself.

SOUL MATES

Have you ever met someone and felt deeply comfortable with him or her, even though you didn't know the person very well? The bond is instant and easy and usually feels like positive family love. That's a soul mate.

Soul mates are members of your soul family. Often you have incarnated with these beings before. You know them on some level. They are family. Although life is one big giant family anyway, souls often repeatedly experience existence together in *soul groups*. In your human lives, these are your soul mates.

Soul mates may show up in your life as family members, friends, or romantic partners. They can make great friends and sometimes great life partners, depending on what agreements were made between you prior to incarnating.

Soul mates even occasionally show up as rivals or challenging people in your life. They push your buttons and encourage you to grow as a person. They may challenge you, sometimes playing the role of the difficult salesperson who yells at you or the ex who double-crossed you. Although not always pleasant, you have agreed to have these growth experiences and your soul mates are there to play tough roles in your life. In these cases, you may not be close with these people. And that is okay. Sometimes you are not meant to be.

As romantic partners, soul mates can be there to play out karma that you have both agreed to clear, as discussed in Chapter 8. When the karmic fuel burns out and the relationship has become simply an ember of soul connection, the romance is done.

Some soul mate romances become lifelong and can be happy and productive partnerships. Some of these are positive karmic relationships and some can be life enhancing for the long-term. Many happily married couples are soul mates.

These could be spiritual people who remember their lives together prior to the current one where they are romantic partners. Sometimes people are soul mates and twin flames, too.

TWIN FLAMES

Imagine that within each person there is a sacred flame burning, made not of fire but of spirit. It is light at its highest manifestation. In some people it burns in the belly, in some the solar plexus, and in many it burns right in the heart—the center of the chest. Wherever it is, this flame is your spark of divine individuality. It shapes you and guides you. It is your connection to the divine within. If you had a cosmic twin somewhere out there in the universe, his flame might be the same or similar. He might be your twin flame.

Mythology and popular culture provide lots of variations on the twin flame concept, and this book will suggest another. Envision that each being's sacred flame has a complementary flame somewhere with a complementary charge. Like two magnets or two sides of a coin, there is an opposite polarity and yet a mutually enhancing quality to these flames when they are together. They are inexplicably drawn to each other. They enhance each other and inspire each other. There may be more than one twin flame out there for each person.

Often, these flames find each other without trying. Sometimes when they meet, they are harmonious and sometimes they combust. An example of harmony is Jeanne and her husband Micah from Chapter 9. They are twin flames who love each other deeply. Sometimes they push each other's buttons, as twin flames are often wont to do, but most of the time they live in happy harmony.

A client we will call Judy met her twin flame in the form of a female coworker before she met her husband years later. Judy's twin flame was Dallas. They were friends, with no romantic connection. However, it did feel like coming home and meeting your other half in a friend, Judy reports. Over six months Judy and Dallas became very close friends. Then just as suddenly, they combusted in a massive disagreement. It was an explosion of energy! Judy was puzzled for a long time and sought out spiritual coaching from me to make sense of it all. Ultimately, what came out of the experience was an urging from the universe that her other half was out there. She got close with Dallas. It was meant to tell her the real thing was coming soon. The combusting was designed to show her what twin flames sometimes do. Through that process Judy decided to put her intention out to attract her divine complement, if he was on Earth. If not, she asked for a gentle, loving, calm twin flame or soul mate she could live happily and harmoniously with.

DIVINE COMPLEMENTS

Divine complements are twin flames on every level and in every fiber of their beings. To understand the full scope of the divine complement relationship you must first understand lifestreams.

Lifestreams are rays of soul light. They are strandlike fibers of pure soul energy and each one has a specific flavor or quality. Some people have one lifestream and some have many. It is neither better nor worse to have more or fewer lifestreams. It simply is, like red or blue, plums or pears—both good, just different.

Individual rays of soul light, or types of lifestreams, each have a unique essence or flavor. Identical lifestreams can exist in more than one being at a time. In people's energy bodies, if there is more than one lifestream, they group together and form a bundle, like a bundle of electrical wires that are made of light. They are held together in the bundle by the person's soul energy and the person's impetus to incarnate in a physical body. That soul energy serves as a unifying principle, a gravity-like force, and aligns the strands vertically.

The bundle of vertical lifestream strands or a single vertical lifestream are like the spine of the soul body. The soul body is the layer of our energy body that is infused with our soul. It is woven into our physical body with its energetic spine aligned with our physical spine.

The same bundle is duplicated in miniature throughout every cell of the body on an etheric level near the DNA area of the cell. It is like a blueprint for the cell on an energetic level, much like our genes are a blueprint for our bodies on a physical level.

Our soul body also houses our sacred spirit flame (mentioned in the "Twin Flames" section earlier in this chapter). It is made of divine spirit and our lifestream(s). The spine-like lifestream(s) make up the "skeleton" of the soul flame and the divine spirit fire burns around it.

For a person who contains more than one lifestream, a twin flame may have one or more lifestreams in common and so their total flames are similar. They are not always exact, total twins.

People sometimes add lifestreams to their beings. This often occurs without their knowledge. It typically occurs due to spiritual expansion and emotional growth on a profound level. It is not a novel process, but a sacred act of soul growth that does happen. When this happens, relationships are affected only if (1) it is a divine complement relationship and therefore, as we discuss more below, both people eventually end up adding the same lifestreams, or (2) the person who adds the lifestream grows as a person so immensely that their relationship needs to grow immensely too or be outgrown.

Each lifestream has a complement twin lifestream; it is the lifestream's twin flame. There are duplicate lifestreams in different people and the same number of complementary twin lifestreams will exist, always. This is Natural Law.

Divine complements each have the exact same lifestreams fully integrated into their beings. Human beings who are divine complements and are partnered with each other romantically and for the long term sometimes add new lifestreams. In time, their divine complement adds them as well. At those times, they are not exact matches but are so close that the energy and aligned dharma of divine complements remains. These beings have a soul agreement to partner as divine complements and so their soul growth process is supported by that. In that case, it is a given that the other person will "catch up" with lifestream additions.

An obvious example in popular culture of divine complements coming together played out under the close scrutiny of the paparazzi. Angelina Jolie and Brad Pitt had a dramatic beginning literally subjected to the bright lights of the camera. While making the movie *Mr. & Mrs. Smith* they met and felt the magnetic pull of divine complements that meet at the right time (even though with them it may not have *seemed* like the right time) and place and have made a soul agreement to join forces. As is often the case, they have gone on to live their lives in alignment with each other and to contribute a great deal of service to the planet.

That is a common characteristic of divine complements: enhanced dharmic or life's purpose world service lived with great joy.

Characteristics of Divine Complements

Other characteristics of divine complements who meet at the right time and place include:

- Strong telepathy with each other (also occurs with some soul mates and twin flames)
- Similar likes and dislikes (but not all the same)
- Similar life philosophies
- Similar values
- Balanced differences that support their life together and gender roles
- Extrasensory empathy for the other's feelings
- Deeply passionate connection
- Romantic and general compatibility
- Ability to "push the other's buttons" a bit to highlight any learning needed
- Deep instinctual understanding of each other
- Uncanny insight into each other's character and personality
- General life alignment
- An eventual shared and/or complementary life's mission or dharma

- Easy and almost instant energetic chakra alignment and entrainment
- A knowing upon meeting that the connection between them is unlike any other they have experienced
- A partnership mentality that easily appears once they are together
- Psychic and emotional alignment
- A mutually remembered psychic connection with each other before meeting
- An almost immediate readiness to commit to each other for life
- Ability to "see" each other in great detail and with great compassion
- Ability to helpfully assist each other in deep-seated healing
- Deep, undeniable support for each other through all types of ups and downs
- Heightened positive experiences when together (includes fun, passion, and joy)

Divine complements usually magnetize each other at the perfect time and not before. Typically, both people are ready and mature enough (regardless of age) to be together as mostly harmonious romantic life partners.

People can, in theory, have more than one divine complement but will not meet as romantic partners unless the circumstances and their maturity levels are aligned. Sometimes we meet divine complements as other types of people in our lives we feel a connection with. If our intuitive senses are well honed, we can often tell who they are, but not always. Souls who have consistently done their spiritual and emotional work are usually the ones who meet their divine complements and become romantic partners during their lives.

Rainbow Blaze and Dave, Continued

Remember Rainbow Blaze and Dave from Chapter 5? They had an amazing first date where everything aligned. As their love story went on, it continued in a loving and smooth way. There were challenges when they integrated their existing families. Each had children, some of whom were still at home, and the cohabitation was a bit like the Brady Bunch at times. But overall, everything was lovely and harmonious. Rainbow and Dave were so grateful to have found each other! They had felt each other's presence for a long time but both had a lot of emotional baggage to work through. They were diligent and met during their fourth decades on Earth. Both felt proud of their efforts to grow and happy to see the results before them, in the form of each other, divine complements living as eventual husband and wife. Their wedding was beautiful, with all of the kids and family at a lush estate in Connecticut overlooking a pond with flowers all around. The setting was peaceful and colorful, just like their union. Because they were spiritual divine complements, the ceremony was special and sacred to them in a deeply personal way. Everyone there was moved and the party that followed was at once raucous and elegant and completely joy-filled.

DIVINE COMPLEMENTS COMING TOGETHER ALL OVER THE WORLD

Before you can meet your divine complement, you may have to do some emotional growth and processing and also undergo a general purging of old baggage. The forces of light and evolutionary blessing create opportunities for growth and clearing. Then, if both you and your complement engage in this process, these same benevolent forces will point you two in the direction of each other. If the circumstances are right, you are ready, and things line up, you will meet. Alignment includes any necessary personal emotional, mental, and spiritual growth. Your internal house will need to be in order and so will his. These factors help line you both up to meet.

An example is Mary. She finally went into therapy and worked through some long-term patterns she had played out in prior relationships. Once those were cleaned up, she and her therapist had Mary's adoptive dad come to therapy with her and rework some old patterns to more healthfully create their relationship. The week they finished therapy, discharged with flying colors, she met her divine complement Jeremy. Everything lined up.

Sometimes near misses happen before the actual meeting. These near misses serve different functions: heart opening, energetically revving you up, getting you mentally prepared, and more. Janet met John at a conference about sound healing. They became fast friends. During the week-long conference, the two of them were in a group hiking through the high desert in New Mexico. They hiked as a loose group and up front were Janet and John. They came to a gate. It was heavy and John opened it for Janet. Something happened energetically to Janet as she walked through. She felt an opening in her heart, and inexplicably, the urge to cry. After the conference, Janet wondered if John was her divine complement even though the friendship had been platonic. She was feeling so much, as if her heart had been dormant and now it was alive again. Lots of old stored emotion flowed forth in the weeks following the conference. In opening that gate John had metaphorically opened something up in Janet. She worked through it and rode that wave as best as she could. It completed and within two months Janet met Will, whom she later married. Her heart was opened by her friendship with John and she understood it was a necessary step on her road to eventually meeting Will, her divine complement.

Remember, *everything* is working together to line you up with your divine complement. The reason benevolent helper forces are urging divine complements to come together all over the world is simple: It is good for the planet. When divine complements are together they provide a level of loving support and understanding for each other that allows them to eventually spread their wings and soar. This raises the vibration of the planet and betters the Earth-reality.

In addition, when divine complements are together and their auras (the electromagnetic fields of energy that surround their bodies) are touching, their auras grow. These fields actually grow larger and more luminous. This brings more universal life force energy into the atmosphere, which also raises the vibration of the planet. Everybody wins! Every life form on Earth benefits when the planet's vibration is raised.

ASKING FOR WHAT YOU WANT

There are numerous helpful spirit beings available to assist you in getting ready for, and then meeting, your divine complement. Just ask! Most helpful beings can get involved only if you ask them directly. A good start is to ask any beings you have felt drawn to for help. For example, any Archangels or goddesses, such as Aphrodite and Isis, can help, as well as angels who are specific Divine Complement Angels. You can ask for them in general terms; you need not know their names.

You can communicate with helpful beings in endless ways. Two suggestions follow:

1. Talk out loud to the being as you would a friend. Listen with your inner ears for a response; it may arrive as an event in your life or in your dreams at night.
2. Write a letter to her/him.

WRITE A LETTER TO A SPIRIT HELPER

Write like you would write a letter to a friend. Ask any questions you have about her/him, preparing for your divine complement, your life, or the nature of existence. The helpful being will delight in your communication and in answering your questions. Write and ask for advice or write just to talk and get to know each other. You can ask for any help you may need or want in any given situation. Build a relationship with her/him.

Sign your letter, fold it up, place it under your pillow or in your pillowcase, and sleep on it. When you write a letter to a specific being and sleep on it, it is an invitation for the being to visit you in your dreams. This being can become a trusted friend, a teacher, and even a confidant. Get to know each other.

DIVINE COMPLEMENTS IN REAL TIME

Call me idealistic, but I believe that divine complements are finding each other more frequently than ever. Does everybody have one that they have the potential of meeting? I'm not sure. I hope so. I think everyone does. I do think there is a chance that some of our divine complements are not in physical bodies when we are. If that is the case, then what should a spiritual dater who is looking for hers do? The answer: trust.

Trust that life is perfect. If for some reason your divine complement is not here yet, if you are meant to meet him, he will arrive. Somehow.

TRUST IN THE DIVINE

I will let you in on a secret that may seem a bit out there. Before I met my divine complement, I worked through my issues with diligence, and I had a lot to work through. It took time and I became impatient. I missed him in some ways, even though we'd yet to meet. I am clairvoyant and so I sometimes converse with my spirit guides or helpers. One day I asked about this topic and lamented, was he even here on Earth? Was he ready? Would he be emotionally ready when I was? I had so many questions. My helpers said, "When you are ready, if your divine complement is not ready or won't soon be, one of us will come down there and manifest an adult body and be your divine complement." I was floored. First, I felt the truth of how much our guides really love us in those words. Second, I understood that if I was ready and wanted it, if the timing was right, it would really happen and nothing could stop it. That let me relax about it and just live my life. For me it worked out; my guy was ready before me! So it was just a matter of synchronistic circumstances drawing us together at the proper time.

PATTY AND JOHN

Patty and her divine complement, John, met online. They were both second-time-arounders. Both had been married years before. John was a well-respected meditation coach and Patty was spiritual in her private life. They both worked through a lot of issues: emotional, mental, and spiritual. Both were compelled to go online and join the same dating site. They found each other there and it was a coming home. Seeing them together was witnessing a glorious, radiant reunion! Everyone around them was uplifted. Years later, they are still deeply in love. Yes, they push each other's buttons sometimes. They live in harmony, though, and went on an extended travel to see the world together for over a year. They, too, found each other at the right time after both had wondered if it would ever really happen for them. It did.

TIMING AND PATIENCE

When you want something now, the last thing you want to hear is to be patient and trust divine timing. But that is what I have to tell you. Although we'd like to know when and how it will happen so we can prepare for it, it is usually meant to be a surprise. It will be a surprise whether your perfect, true love mate is a soul mate, a twin flame, a divine complement, or some combination of the three. Just know, whoever he is, he is coming. There will be someone for you. Hold high standards for yourself and your mate. Rest in the knowledge that you are sacred and let that be your guide.

Timing is your friend. It will make your life work out just right. Trust it.

Patience will ease your journey. Enjoy your life in the present moment, and be full.

REST IN YOUR SACREDNESS

1. Breathe deeply and state aloud, "I am sacred."
2. Now from your heart, letting your mind rest, state that you are resting in your sacredness and faith knowing the best will happen for you in your love life. Here is an example of what you can say, "I trust that as I rest in my sacredness, I will effortlessly draw to me the perfect mate and he will be my true love. I allow myself to heal and work through any necessary issues with ease and send a blessing that he may do the same. I trust life to bring me goodness in perfect timing."
3. Notice whether you feel more patient than before. You may or not. Either way is okay. You have put your intention out and looked at a lot of your issues in this book

already. You are probably very close to being ready, or are ready. Trust is your buzzword now.

BELIEVING IN GOODNESS

The universe is designed to be a positive place. Having a positive outlook and believing in goodness help you to do two things:

- Attract your true love partner.
- Feel patient and happy before and after he comes into your life.

Believing in goodness pervades your life. If you feel it and expect it, it will show up in all areas of your life: romantic, career, home, social, everywhere. Put your focus on the positive. Talk about it. Make a commitment to speak positively 90 percent of the time. Focus on the good stuff.

DO YOU BELIEVE?

Is goodness your reality? Do you want it to be? Truly ask yourself, do you focus on everything that is wrong with your life? Could you list everything that is right?

1. Do it now. Make a list of all that is right in your life. There should be a lot! Don't go the sob story route and tell yourself all the reasons things aren't right. Instead, focus on all the goodness, the reasons things are right.
2. Make a commitment to exert mental discipline on yourself, not only stopping yourself from making negative comments but even from thinking negatively.

3. Write your commitment down. Is it to make at least thirty positive comments per day? To spend five minutes each morning in the mirror telling yourself all the positive things in your life or all the reasons you are awesome? Come up with a commitment you are willing to make.

Do you want to believe in goodness? By believing in goodness what do you have to give up—what limiting beliefs or behavioral habits?

1. Make a list of those limiting beliefs or habits—things you say or do that get in the way of your believing in goodness.
2. Look at your list. Are you willing to let go of all that blocks your infinite goodness?
3. If yes, state that willingness aloud. Remember, your cells hear you and do what you ask of them. State, "I choose goodness and joy as the all-pervasive forces in my life. I choose to live as my Higher Self and be love. I accept goodness and believe in the beauty of life. It is done."

Make a conscious choice to believe in goodness and let it come to you. Trust divine timing, even if you don't understand it sometimes. Let your life be easy.

A major part of the dance to meet your true love is about you believing in goodness. All of the information about soul mates, twin flames, and divine complements is here to give you ideas and a view toward the reality you want to create. You are the architect of your reality and you can be conscious and prepare yourself for your true love to arrive in your life at the perfect time.

Chapter Twelve
It's Always All about You!

Everything about you creates your reality. Your thoughts, feelings, actions, and heart all shape the life you live. Your entire being informs your world and how you experience it. Your outer life is an expression of everything inside of you. When you accept this truth, you start owning your life.

Ownership of your life and by extension yourself allows something powerful to happen. You are no longer in the position of the victim, to whom life just happens. Instead you are the creator, the one who orchestrates your world. Then there is no one else to blame your faults and pitfalls on. You have to accept yourself, as you are. Seem a little scary? Self-acceptance is pure power. It liberates you! No longer are you not good enough, or your life not good enough, because you are negatively impacted by other's choices. You take the reins. You hold all the cards.

This chapter is all about taking ownership of you. By recognizing how wonderful you are, and by treating yourself (and your world) with lovingkindness, you can create a dating life that fulfills you and brings you great joy. The keys that make a great date come from inside of you! Your self-love, your self-acceptance, your ability to be present in the moment and even your ability to trust yourself are ingredients that not only serve up an amazing date, they also serve up a fabulous life. Start gathering up these ingredients now by reading on.

LETTING GO OF ANGER: MEN ARE NOT THE ENEMY

Are you a little bit angry at most men? I know I was and I'm still working on it. Sometimes it is so low-grade or far under the surface that we don't know it's even there. There are a lot of reasons to feel angry and irritated at the male gender in general: poor treatment by jerky guys we've dated; cheating by a man we loved; crimes against women perpetrated by men; the way some men objectify us, personally by staring at our chests or generally by ogling porn.

But here is the thing. Not all guys are like that. And to truly accept a man who does come into your life you're going to have to let go of that general anger at the male population, 'cause your true love is one of them.

Sometimes our generally negative view of the male population comes out in subtle ways. Do you find yourself automatically blaming the guy when you hear of a couple's love story gone wrong? In the world of girl talk I'd tell you, "Yeah, it probably is the dude's fault." But really, if I didn't know, maybe I could reserve my low opinion of men and not pass judgment. It is easy to blame guys. But it is definitely a small percentage of the whole that gives the rest of them a very bad rap.

So, as always, it comes back to you. You choose to be distrustful of guys. Using your discernment is key here. Sometimes you aren't feeling trusting because your instincts are telling you something and sometimes it might be a general bias against men.

An example of instincts cuing you in to trouble is when you hear all about a friend's guy and can tell he doesn't see her as the amazing goddess she is. He is shifty, distant, often absent. She feels insecure and is having a hard time trusting him. You meet him and he doesn't look you in the eye. You can just tell. He isn't good enough for your friend. Your instincts will tell you.

An example of general anti-guy bias is when your date leaves all the dishes in the sink after you cooked him dinner at your house. He doesn't clean up. You automatically conclude that he should have loaded the dishwasher, he may be lazy, he won't pull his weight later. You blame him and think negatively of him. The truth might be that he didn't feel comfortable commandeering your kitchen yet. Or he didn't see the dishes in there. Sometimes we all jump to the worst possible conclusions, especially about guys.

You can consciously choose to be positive and at the same time to discern with clarity. Men are not the enemy. Most of them are wonderful people. And some of them are true loves to all kinds of amazing spiritual, sexy women out there, including you.

LOVING THE PRESENT MOMENT

Sometimes we make the mistake of living in the future or the past, harping on all of the past events that we are not over or focusing on the future, thinking, "I'll be happier when I find my soul mate or a new job or move to a new town." But spiritual dating is about living in the present. Living in the now, not putting off your life until tomorrow or next year. To spiritually date, you have to be present.

To be in the moment, present, is a peak experience. Think of the transcendent moments in your life. Some examples might be parasailing high above the sea in total quiet, watching the birth of a baby, coasting down a gentle hill on your bike, swimming underwater with dolphins and fish, when you got the news that something you created was being shared and loved by many, when a butterfly landed on your arm and stayed there for minutes, when you hit a winning home run in softball, or when a deer looked you deeply in the eyes while you shared space. During a transcendent moment, you are 100 percent present.

Remember that feeling of being completely there with no extraneous thoughts, no to-do lists floating around in your mind? You were just in the moment, loving that moment. That makes sense— when you are experiencing something amazing, beautiful, or moving, you want to savor it.

Can you imagine what it would be like to be that present for even a small part of your life? You'd really listen fully during that time. You would taste and feel and sense every moment when you are that present. On a date, you would be so with it, so real, so there. Imagine that level of authenticity on a date and in your life. In this way, you would really know your date on a deeper level than if you were just half-listening and thinking about touching up your lipstick in the bathroom after dessert.

Being present is all about you. It is about being totally with who you are and fully in your skin. You are in your body, not dissociating and averting your eyes from the moment. It improves your life to be present. Your life will be more authentic and true in this way. It will be more real.

HOW TO BE PRESENT
Use this exercise to help bring your wandering mind to the present moment.

1. Sit in a comfortable seat and relax your mind.

- Breathe and be still.
- Feel your heart beat.
- Notice the breath moving in and out of your body.
- Feel your body relax.
- Let your heart know it can be felt and seen now. It can stop hiding.

- Now state, "I choose to be present to the moment and in my authentic truth. My heart is free in each moment."
- Now sit, breathe, and meditate, clearing your mind gently. If thoughts come up, just witness them from an unattached place. They are like high clouds scuttling quickly past on a breeze, here one moment, gone the next.
- Notice how it feels to be present.
- You are *holding space* for yourself. When you hold space, you allow for effortless healing and easy self-correction. This is happening now with no effort from you except being present. How does it feel?

2. Stay present for as long as feels right. If you repeat this exercise and practice being present you can build up the amount of time you stay present. You will gain clarity of mind, peace of heart, and calmness of body while holding space for your own healing.

Being present on a date allows magic to happen. True connection can form only when you are present. And that is magic, indeed. Two people, in truth, connecting, is a gift. Whether your date is your soul mate or not you will be getting great practice being truly present. Be aware that people are drawn to those who are present to them. In being so present and authentic, you are going to amp up your magnetism, especially your magnetism for the right people. So, get ready.

Being present will aid you on your journey. It will help you remain in lovingkindness toward yourself and others. It will get you through tough times because you can be present to yourself and it will sweeten the goodness because you are more fully experiencing it. Embrace your presence with love.

FAITH IN LOVE = FAITH IN YOURSELF

To truly seek your spiritual soul mate, you have to believe in love. You have to feel deep within you that it does exist and it is real. Love is made of spirit. Spirit/god/goddess/great spirit/source are love. That is why one step you can take is to experience love in the form of spirit. This can help you believe in love, and to have faith in love.

Experience the divine through meditation, shamanism, a church service that resonates with you, a spiritually focused yoga class, a sufi whirling demonstration. Experience the divine within you and you will touch love.

Next, have faith in your self-love. Believe that it is real and authentic and that it will grow. (It will.) Earlier in the book, you learned how to set your intention to validate and grow your self-love. Reaffirm that intention.

Finally, believe in romantic, soul mate love. Is it out there for you? Do you have faith that it is? It is natural to doubt on this path and to question whether the spiritual soul mate love you seek is going to happen for you. The truth is that there is no guarantee—and that is why you must have faith. You have to wait and be surprised. That is the way of things. But I will tell you this: When you are ready, someone else who is perfect for you is going to be ready, too. And all of the forces in the universe are going to get behind you both and urge you together. Count on it. It is a fact.

Spiritual mates are meant to find each other. If you hold out for that and don't settle, it will happen eventually—but you have to have faith in divine timing. You have to trust life.

QUINN'S FAITH

Quinn had decided that she was ready to meet her spiritual soul mate. She had worked through her old patterns, changed her negative attitude toward men, identified her past red flags. Years went by and Quinn managed her bookshop in a quiet English countryside town. She dated gently and carefully, being kind to herself and others. Quinn did everything right as far as spiritual dating went. Yet still, no man came.

One morning, she awoke from a dream with the certainty that she needed to sell her bookshop and move her quiet English countryside life to America. Not just anywhere in America, but California! Sun, sand, skimpy clothes. All were foreign to Quinn's quiet, gentle persona. She knew with the same certainty this was the right move, just as she had known it was the right move to start her bookshop and to make her very lucrative investments.

Four short months later, everything was sold for the highest prices—her business, her cottage, her car. She was off to her new home. She settled in. It was exciting and very different but she had faith in her intuition; it had never led her wrong. And her faith in love remained as did her faith in herself.

She got out there and explored. In a synchronistic conversation in a bookshop, she met a movie director who ended up offering her a job on a film that was a book adaptation. If there was one thing Quinn knew, it was books and writing. She ended up rewriting the entire screenplay. More gigs writing screenplays followed and again Quinn was making money hand over fist and investing it perfectly.

On one of those films she met an actor who had just a few lines. He was basically the British man-candy for the film. Very handsome. Very proper off camera. James. They became friends and spent hours together talking and laughing several times per week. They had similar spiritual views and sensibilities because they were from neighboring towns.

Quinn's nights were happily haunted with images of James. He was in her dreams every night. She decided she had to tell him.

After work one evening they went to dinner and Quinn was fully prepared to bare her soul and take a chance on love. She didn't get the chance. He told her first! He said she was the woman he'd always dreamed of and he loved her. Did she feel the same?

Of course she did and the happily-ever-after goes on from there. Quinn wrote an original screenplay that was nominated for an Oscar and James became better known as an actor. He worked steadily with supporting and starring roles for many years. Blissfully, they lived as husband and wife. Both had kept the faith for many years prior to finding each other, Quinn for over forty years and James for almost forty. They both believed in love and it came to them perfectly at the right time.

HOW TO BELIEVE IN LOVE

Are you a bit skeptical about real love? This exercise will help you find your faith. Have a pen and paper or journal handy to write some thoughts and feelings down.

1. Place your hand on your heart. Feel it. Honor it.

- Why are you worthy of love? List all the reasons, such as that you are made of love and spirit, you try to be a good person, etc.
- What is lovable about you? List at least thirty things! Some examples are: I am cuddly and affectionate. I like football and play it well. I try to grow every day.
- Do you have faith that you deserve a loving partner? That you will be a great addition to that man's life? If yes, then state it aloud to tell your body and its love magnet, "I have faith that life will bring my true love, soul mate partner to me at the perfect time. I believe in love and know that my true love and I will enhance each other's lives in joyful and

beautiful ways. I have faith in love and myself." If no, go back over why you are so lovable and expand your list. Then say the affirmation above anyway. Also, repeat, "I am amazingly lovable. I have faith that I deserve and will have a wonderful loving partner." Say that daily until you believe it.

- Learn from your past. Maybe "love" hasn't seemed so kind to you, leaving you with a broken heart, a messy divorce, maybe even serious debt. Here is the question: Are any of the messes supposedly created by love really messes? Did you learn from them? And most importantly, were they created by your choices: to date the guy who broke your heart, to marry the man with issues, to run up your credit card supporting your boyfriend? Maybe love didn't create those situations; you did. Let love off the hook and take responsibility for your choices. You have the ability to make better ones. Love is an energy that flows through everything and enlivens our hearts. You discern what to do with it.

2. Let your faith in love return and expand. State, "I choose to live love and believe in love's infinite power. I take responsibility for my choices."

TRUSTING YOURSELF WITH LOVE

The spirit of lovingkindness asks you to love yourself and to do it kindly. Part of that is trusting yourself with love, trusting that you are worthy of being loved. However, lovingkindness also means learning to trust yourself with someone else's love. When someone loves you, it is a vulnerable place for them to be. You can hurt them if you aren't careful or don't love them back.

PAULINE LEARNS ABOUT TRUST

Pauline was not one to get into serious relationships very often. As a result, around the two-month mark, she often ended things with suitors. Some were crushed and a few even said they loved her and really thought their relationships with her were going somewhere. Pauline was a lover and she put her whole being into things while she was in them. And she knew when it was time to exit. She felt bad that she hurt those men, but rationalized that that was why she always ended it early—to hurt them less. She was just trying to be real and authentic. If she couldn't see a future with them, she tried to set them free as quickly as possible.

You Are Never Alone

All around you, every day, are loving helpful energies. Some people might call them spirit guides, some divine energy. Whatever they are to you, the love that surrounds you is palpable if you allow yourself to feel it. You are actually being wrapped in lovingkindness in each moment.

Accept this love now by stating your intention aloud: "I gratefully accept all the love and support offered to me by all of the helpful, benevolent energies in my life. I honor my spirit guides, and all of the divine energy of love and light that is available to me with my whole heart. Thank you. I receive your love and support now and forever more. So be it."

When she started dating Jeff, she knew it was different this time. She felt more—more love, more passion, more of everything, in a totally real and completely authentic way. As the two-month mark approached, she got nervous. Jeff was such a special person. She didn't want to hurt him. She wasn't sure if she could trust herself with his love. What if she hurt him? What if she decided she had to leave?

One weekend while he was on a business trip, she took the time to work through this. She looked at her feelings for him. She already couldn't imagine her life without him. She realized there was no way she would voluntarily leave such a wonderful man. Pauline made a conscious decision to trust herself with Jeff's love and vowed that if she ever needed to end it, she would do so with lovingkindness and that was the best she could do.

Pauline forgave herself for ending all the previous relationships that were not right for her. She honored that she didn't settle for something that wasn't right and because of that she found Jeff. Pauline made peace with her past and honored her future, whatever it held.

KATIE BEGINS TO BELIEVE

Katie was born to drug-addicted parents. Her childhood home life was filled with their parties where they made meth and used crack—very heavy stuff. At fifteen, Katie left home with aspirations to become a ballet dancer. She ended up dancing in a strip club for eight years. Things that went on there were worse than you can imagine. At twenty-three, she was able to turn her life around. She went to school and got her MBA. A job in finance followed. She excelled and was repeatedly promoted. Eventually, at age thirty, she was named junior vice president. The meteoric rise at her job let Katie, thankfully, leave her past behind her.

But she had a secret. No one could know what she had been. And she had zero interest in dating. To her men were kind of gross. All the things she saw and lived in her past were too much. For a long time she was content with not dating and staying very busy. Between work and some friends she'd made, her life felt full.

One Saturday, she saw a loving couple strolling hand-in-hand and her heart woke up just a little bit. She might want that kind of companionship. As she felt that, all kinds of intense images and feelings flooded her body. She realized she needed help. She couldn't manage what she'd seen and experienced alone. She entered psychotherapy. Lots of work followed, for years. When I met Katie she had done so much healing, she just needed help clearing her body of residual energies.

As that process and her psychotherapy went on, one day Katie came to an experiential realization; she *did* deserve goodness. She said she'd never felt that before. She certainly never believed it. Eventually, she could say and truly feel in her bones, "I deserve the best. I deserve goodness and love and happiness and peace. I really do." Her body responded and let go of more heavy energy when she uttered those words and believed them.

Years later, Katie has dated a bit and now has a loving boyfriend she feels safe with. She doesn't hide her past from him. She accepts herself as best as she can and Rory, her guy, completely accepts her. Katie still has issues come up from time to time. Her early trauma was pretty intense and it is natural for things to arise. When she needs to, she sees her psychotherapist or gets herself energy healing. She continues to integrate that she truly deserves the best.

THE BEST FOR YOU

What constitutes "the best" for you? Getting (or deserving) the best is not just getting what you want. It is asking your full being, body, mind, heart, spirit, soul what is truly best, for your highest good. Let's ask your being now.

1. Relax, breathe, and feel into your heart. Now state, "I allow my body and being to communicate with me now. No judgments, I accept what you have to say."

   - What is the best, the most wonderful ideal, for you in the arena of your career? What feeling do you feel when you do your work?
   - Next, what is the best for you in the arena of your home life? What does it look and feel like? Who is there?
   - What is best for your love life? What does that feel like? Look or sound like? Smell like?
   - What is best for how you spend your time? Ask your body and being to show you.
   - Now ask your body to communicate anything that you need to know. Are there any impediments to you receiving the best? Be open to your body's answers.

2. Now list what is best for you from this exercise that you are not already living.

Once you've taken stock of what truly is your best, you need to create an intention—and a plan—for making that a reality in your life.

   - First, list the steps you need to take to get to those places and make those situations happen.
   - Next, write down next to each step how long it will take you to achieve that step. Commit to a date by which you will have enacted that step, even if it years away.

Trusting yourself with love is powerful and sometimes requires introspection and self-awareness. You can do it! Remember, you deserve the very best, no matter who you are or where you've been. You are a radiant being of light. That is the truth.

CONCLUSION

Boy, you've done a lot of work! Look how much you've learned about yourself and how much you've grown. You created your Love Life Roadmap in Chapter 4. Use it. Follow it, revise it, add to it, embellish it. You have applied your intent, attention, and focus in a big way throughout the duration of the book. What gets attention gets energy. What gets energy manifests in your physical reality. You did it! And you'll keep doing it.

Be proud of how you have identified your red flags, built up your confidence, made a commitment to be authentic in your life. And most of all, how you have chosen yourself, your happiness, your well-being. I'm really proud of you—I gave you a rigorous personal growth assignment with this book and you ran with it! You rock. Seriously.

I want to remind you one last time before we part ways for the moment how amazing you are. I hope you love yourself more than ever and that self-love keeps growing for the rest of your days. I have faith that you will find your true love in the perfect way at the perfect time. If you are ever short on that faith, borrow a little of mine. Because mine is boundless. I really believe that there is a wonderful true love match out there for all of us, you included. We need to prepare ourselves, do our emotional and spiritual work to get ready, and know that the amount of work we do is directly proportional to the quality of guy we will end up with. Don't skimp on the emotional and spiritual growth. It is an investment in your future happiness.

Open your heart. Every day. Open your heart. Surround the Earth with your love. Live with the beautiful, authentic truth inside your heart. Radiate it outward and fill yourself with it. Believe in love and yourself. Believe in how incredible you are and believe that life will bring you an incredible true love to share your life together at just the right time in just the right way.

Accept the goodness and love that life has to offer you. Every moment is a gift from life to you. View your world with positive, rose-colored, love-filled glasses. See the loving child hugging her puppy on the street and let that love in. Let the loving child inside of you reawaken and feel the freedom of your existence. You are the architect. You are the creator, the artist who designs your life. Put your full focus on making a great life for yourself. You deserve it. You are worthy of happiness, health, love, light, all the goodness in the world.

You are never truly alone. You always have a huge host of loving energies all around you. Life, spirit, divinity, god, goddess, great mystery, great spirit—whatever you call universal life force loves you SO deeply and completely. From this benevolent presence you are accepted, held, cared for, nurtured. Life is rooting for you. Rooting for you to get the great job, the great guy, have the happy life. All of it. You just need to believe in it. Affirm it and it will be so.

Trust life, trust yourself, trust your beautiful, radiant heart, and let your life be easy.

INDEX

for sacred dating, 107

Interconnection, 156, 160

Intercourse, 137. *See also* Sex

Intimacy, 171

Intuition, 96, 125–27, 133

Joy, 11, 38–41, 69–70, 139–40

Karma, 156–62, 205

Kindness, 111

Kissing, 175–76

Law of Three, 14

Letting go, 24–26

Licking, 175–76

Lifestreams, 207–08

Love

in childhood, 154

craving, 70

faith in, 224–27

opening to, 42–43

replacing fear with, 163–65

true, 130–31, 203–04

trusting yourself with, 227–29

Love life

defining your, 80–81

envisioning future, 81–82, 88–89

Love Life Roadmap, 61, 85–89

Lovemaking, 137, 144–45. *See also* Sex

Lovingkindness, 201, 227

Loving perfection, 3

Magnetism, 58–60, 61, 223

Male life energy, 187–88

Mediocre relationships, 162

Memories, body, 31–32

Men

hara energy of, 190

letting go of anger toward, 220–21

Mental needs, 84

Money-magnetism, 139

Mother issues, 153–54

Mutual recognition, 193–94

Natural law, 13–15, 208

Needs

emotional, 68–71, 83–84

About the Author

Amy Leigh Mercree honed her intuitive skills, while in college earning her teaching degree, with an extensive apprenticeship in Native American Style Medicine Healing. While working as a school teacher at age twenty-two she began her path as a healer.

As a practicing Medical Intuitive for eleven years, Amy has seen many women and men through illness and emotional healing. She is sure that, using a combination of deep spiritual truths, joyful determination, and perceptive insight, we can all shed our old baggage and emerge into the light of love.

Amy became a conscious dating coach after watching clients struggle with relationships for years. She noticed that women needed to be strongly empowered and reminded how special, sacred, and unique they were. Her life's mission evolved into helping her clients and readers embrace their sacred selves through self-love and self-awareness.

Her blog *www.spiritualgirlsguide.com* offers spiritual dating and life advice, outrageous and heart-melting dating stories, and an advice column that answers your juiciest dating questions, such as "Is there a spiritual reason my crush on a coworker is so strong? It is a sexual obsession!" and "How do I get over a perceived love of my life that dumped me?"

Do you have a dating story to share? Have you experienced dating disasters or success stories? Do you have some advice for other spiritual daters based on your story? Send it to *Stories@spiritualgirlsguide.com*. Do you have a question about spiritual dating, conscious versus unconscious dating, or a dating dilemma? Send it to *askamy@spiritualgirlsguide.com* and it may be anonymously answered on the blog!

If you have any other questions or are interested in Conscious Dating Coaching, you can write to Amy at either of the e-mail addresses listed above.

ON TOP

Getting Where Women Really Belong

- Trying to lose the losers you've been dating?
- Striving to find the time to be a doting mother, dedicated employee, and still be a hot piece of you-know-what in the bedroom?
- Been in a comfortable relationship that's becoming, well, too comfortable?

Don't despair! Visit the Jane on Top blog—your new source for information (and commiseration) on all things relationships, sex, and the juggling act that is being a modern gal.